NC

The Scrum that Changed my Life

SWANSEA LIBRARIES

6000181900

The Scrum that Changed my Life

Bryan Davies
and Elfyn Pritchard

First impression: 2013

© Copyright Bryan Davies and Y Lolfa Cyf., 2013

The contents of this book are subject to copyright, and may
not be reproduced by any means, mechanical or electronic,
without the prior, written consent of the publishers.

Thanks to the
Welsh Rugby Charitable Trust,
Registered Charity No. 502079
www.wrct.org.uk
for financially supporting the publication of this book

ISBN: 978 184771 6927

Published and printed in Wales
on paper from well maintained forests by
Y Lolfa Cyf., Talybont, Ceredigion SY24 5HE
website www.ylolfa.com
e-mail ylolfa@ylolfa.com
tel 01970 832 304
fax 832 782

Bryan (Yogi) Davies

1957–2013

Contents

CHAPTER 1

In the Scrum

i

SATURDAY, 21 APRIL 2007, a date engraved on my mind for ever, the day that changed my life, and one that neither I nor my family will ever forget. A balmy spring day, but greeted in newspapers with banner headlines:

> Rugby dad's horror injury in final match
> Rugby dad has suspected broken neck
> Crippled by scrum

And this is how the local paper *Y Cyfnod* chronicled the event (in Welsh):

> It is feared that a local rugby player who promised to play one last game has broken his neck. Bryan Davies (Yogi as he is known) 49 years old, has been a Bala player for over 20 years...
>
> 'The accident happened during the first scrum, five minutes into the match' said Gwyndaf Hughes, the club secretary. 'I think Bryan realised immediately what had happened – his first words were – "don't move me, I'm in trouble".'

English newspapers were even more dramatic. This is part of the report which appeared in the Welsh edition of the *Daily Post*:

> **Player's injury horror in last game for club**
> A rugby playing dad suffered a suspected broken neck during his last match for the club he represented for more than 20 years. Bryan Davies told team mates in the dressing room before Saturday's match that he was playing his last ever game for Bala Rugby Club. And to mark the occasion the 49 year old was handed the captaincy.
>
> But within minutes of the Asda League Four North clash against

Nant Conwy getting under way a scrum collapsed and the dad-of-two was left with serious back injuries.

...It is understood Mr Davies has no feeling in the lower part of his body and doctors fear he may never walk again. '...They have more or less said the chances of him walking again are slim.

'He is on life support, but only because he has trouble breathing. He is conscious. But it's difficult to understand what exactly he is telling us. He has done so much for the club and helped so many people.'

We had been a happy, carefree family the previous Wednesday, returning home from the Caribbean after a holiday in the sun; myself, my wife Susan and the children Ilan and Teleri. Whilst there I had come to an important decision, no more first-team rugby with the Bala club, it was high time I retired from the game. Not total retirement perhaps, if the second team asked me to play for them, I would do so, but not the first team. No, this was definitely my last season for them as I was getting too long in the tooth for the hard battles of the first team. I was approaching my 50th birthday and that in a sport where 35 is considered old!

But there remained one fixture, against the old enemy – Nant Conwy from the Conwy Valley. We had enjoyed many a hard battle with them over the years, their style of play being like Bala's, tough and uncompromising, with no one on either side prepared to give an inch. This was a fixture postponed from a previous date, earlier in the season. Then, on the eve of the scheduled match, one of Nant Conwy's players was killed in a road accident on the Padog bends between Betws y Coed and Pentrefoelas, and naturally the game was postponed, and that until the last Saturday of the season, the only date available to both clubs.

To this day flowers, constantly renewed, mark the spot of that tragic accident on the A5.

I was the first-team's hooker, having been previously a prop and prior to that, believe it or not, a centre. The Bala centres then were two Brians, Brian Lloyd the blacksmith from Llanfor and myself, and it so happened that we were related. We were not the fastest runners on the field, but it was difficult to run through us, both of us being so much better in defence than attack.

I played in the centre for two or three seasons, then, because there was a shortage of props, I volunteered for the front eight and became the loose head prop, a position I held for 15 seasons until the 2004–2005 season when our hooker Geraint Llwyn Brain left for Aberystwyth, and the club had no one to take his place, or there was no one crazy enough to volunteer. But I was, thinking it would only be for a couple of matches. But there I remained for the remainder of my playing days, in the most dangerous position on the field. In the scrum the hooker has no hands or arms to defend himself unlike most other players on the field who have at least one arm free.

I have always endeavoured to give of my best, but since self praise is no recommendation I will leave the eulogising to someone else. This is an extract of what was written about me by a member of the Bala club:

> During the last few seasons he became a fierce rival who won respect on every rugby field in north Wales and beyond. Yogi gave of his best in every match and often his immediate opponent suffered the consequences. He had an insatiable appetite for the game and he played with heart and enthusiasm and never voluntarily took a step backwards. He led the pack, inspired his team mates and looked after the young players.

But I digress. When we were all assembled in the changing room for the Nant Conwy match, the last encounter of the season, I told the others that I had decided to hang up my boots, and that this would be my last appearance for the first team. Our captain had been suspended from playing in this fixture and I was immediately given the honour for the day, and it was I who led the team out into the sunshine of Maes Gwyniad. This was my first experience of the captaincy, having successfully avoided that responsibility over the years!

The fixture attracted a good crowd, it being the last match and that against very special opponents in Nant Conwy. After a ferocious opening period came the first scrum on the far side from where most spectators were standing and that is when the accident happened. There was no score but although both teams were evenly matched, things augured well for Bala and there were early signs that we could overcome our opponents and gain a famous victory.

It was a Bala put-in by Euros Jones, our scrum half, and the props were Tom Hughes and Meilir Vaughan Evans.

As those who are well versed in the sport know, dark and secret things happen in the scrum, a fist, a prod, some illegal shoving; everybody at it and the authorities forever striving to devise rules and regulations in an attempt to stamp out this kind of behaviour. We, the members of the pack, often discussed the possibility of serious injury happening to one of us, especially when both packs stood face to face and then ferociously launched themselves at the opponents. This was before the touch, pause, engage ritual which was introduced for this very reason, although this has by now been amended to touch and engage only.

Everyone in the scrum is expected to push straight but this doesn't happen. The opponent's tight head prop will endeavour to push upwards under the opposite hooker's shoulder in order to give their hooker the advantage, and that is what happened on this occasion. At the same time as my left shoulder was being raised by the prop my right shoulder was simultaneously being raised by the hooker, and of course my head was stuck, somewhere between my legs. My head down and my shoulders being raised and solid pushing from both packs, that is what simply – if simple is the word – happened. I heard a crack like a gunshot and I knew in that instant that I had broken my neck. No one else heard anything because the sound waves were travelling through my skull.

Everything happened in an instant. It was the Bala second row who first realised that something was amiss, and they tried to draw back, and naturally, because the weight from our side slackened, the Nant Conwy pack came over us and the scrum collapsed. It was then that the referee blew his whistle to put a stop to things, and when everybody got up, there I was flat on my back, unable to move but conscious of everything that had happened.

Tony Parry, the Bala chairman, was running the line, and Alwyn 'Ambulance', one of the local paramedics, was present in the crowd. They both rushed on to the field and Alwyn positioned my head properly so that no more damage would be caused, and Geraint Fedw Arian held my head to await the ambulance.

It was more than three quarters of an hour before it arrived, having been called out to another incident, and no other ambulances were available in Bala at the time. The air ambulance helicopter arrived at the same time. The referee had stopped his watch when the accident happened, so we can be accurate about the time.

I remember telling Geraint that I had broken my neck and that I felt as if my arms were placed across my chest. I asked him where they were. 'They are down by your side,' he replied. Strangely enough, when I get a bad spell or a spasm, I get terrible pains in my arms and feel that they are placed across my chest. I have been told that these are phantom pains and phantom feelings.

Although not aware of it at the time, normal breathing was impossible, so I was breathing through my stomach, resulting in less oxygen and more carbon dioxide reaching my lungs, causing permanent damage. I was told by one of the doctors in hospital that the prognosis would have been better for me had there been oxygen on the field, but there wasn't and so that was that. My lungs have shrunk and the muscles have deteriorated, that is why I am unable, to this day, to breathe without help.

As I lay there on the field I remember that breathing caused me great pain. I was told later that this was because I had shattered part of my neck, the third, fourth and fifth vertebrae having been destroyed, and the spinal cord trapped between the third and fourth vertebrae.

Both teams were asked to leave the field and the referee came to me and I told him that I had broken my neck. But nobody believed me at the time. The match was abandoned immediately, but the crowd did not disperse, so many individuals in it being concerned about me.

Someone got in touch with Susan, my wife, and she came at once. Before she realised how badly hurt I was she chastised me because my boots looked a sorry sight. I never bothered buying new ones, I repaired the old pair with masking tape, and by now they were more tape than boots. Susan never saw them because they were kept in the boot of the car. She also asked me if my pants were clean.

But when I informed her that I had broken my neck, she was naturally most upset, especially since she remembered my telling her once that if, as a result of illness or an accident, I lost the use of my legs, I would no longer want to live.

When the helicopter arrived I was wrapped up and taken to Wrexham Maelor Hospital, with Susan following in Tony Parry's car. I was taken immediately to the A&E unit where the doctor refused to reveal the extent of my injury. So I told him! I told him that I had a broken neck and he was shocked when he realised that I knew, but maybe I'd had a tougher upbringing than him!

ii

I was born in a council house in Uwchydre, Corwen – 'top town' as we, the children used to call it – and Mam often said that it was very much like Sgubor Goch, a notorious estate in Caernarfon, not that this meant anything to me. But we soon moved to Isydre, the lower side of the town – 'bottom town' – to a house on London Road, the A5, adjacent to the church school. My first memory, and I must have been about three at the time, was of an old man named Tanat – I never knew his full name – who used to come by the house every day at two in the afternoon. I believe that he was a river gamekeeper, and he had three terriers, two at his heels, and one in his bag! He lived in a small council house across the road from us, and he kept the dogs in the house. I would hear them scratching at the door. He would often bring Mam a rabbit or a hare or a pheasant for the pot, and I can still call to mind his long, untidy grey hair. It was he who cut my hair, and would do so by placing a bowl on my head, and cutting round it.

It was in the house on London Road that my sister Joyce was born, so there were four of us: Dad, Mam, me and my sister. Being next door to the school, I used to climb through a hole in the fence to join the children on the school yard every play time. But there was one boy, Dafydd, I don't remember how old he was, who pushed me back every time I climbed through the fence, and that used to break my heart because I couldn't play with the other children.

One day however, Uncle Berwyn came by and saw Dafydd pushing me back through the fence, and he came to me and said: 'The next time he does that to you, show him your right fist, and belt him in the face with your left, that'll hurt him.'

So, full of myself, I went through the fence, and along came Dafydd to push me back. 'Do you see this?' I asked, showing him my right fist, 'Well it's this one that hurts,' and I punched him in the face with my left until he was flat out on the school yard. I had such a fright that I ran back through the fence crying, and there was Uncle Berwyn standing in the doorway laughing. He then told me, 'Never start a fight with anyone, but if someone else wants a fight with you, make sure you finish him off!'

I don't know what became of Dafydd, I don't remember seeing him in primary or secondary school, he must have moved elsewhere, but I can still recall the shock on his face to this day!

My father was a farm labourer at Wernddu, Gwyddelwern, while my mother stayed at home to look after me and my sister. In the early years, Nain, Dad's mother, was with us as well, and I remember thinking that she was a cruel old lady, always saying that little children should be seen and not heard. She often pinched us to keep us quiet.

When I was nearly five, we moved from London Road to a council house, number 74 on the Maesafallen estate – an estate of about a 100 houses on the other side of the River Dee. There, my brother Arwyn was born, and he spent several months in hospital because he only had half a stomach.

The move from one house to the other was made with the aid of a tractor and trailer, as my father never had a car and never had a driving licence, and after some years as a farmhand, he became self-employed, doing several jobs such as selling firewood.

I made friends with several children on the estate, especially Ian, the son of the children's author J Selwyn Lloyd. Ian's father was a teacher at Corwen School, and because of that, none of the other children wanted to be friends with him, and they would pick on him in school, and when that happened, I would go over to interfere!

I remember very little about school, only that I went there on the bus from Maesafallen, that Mr Griffiths was the headmaster and that I soon realised that it wasn't the place for me!

I don't remember who my teachers were at the 'top school' as it was called (because the church school, the one I used to live next to was called – 'bottom school') but the majority were women, and J Selwyn Lloyd, my friend Ian's father taught Standard 5.

I didn't like school at all. To be frank I absolutely hated it, and hated every day that I went there. I disliked the headmaster, Mr Griffiths, who used to slap me with a ruler, although I probably deserved it. I disliked the teachers and all the lessons, except sport and PE.

But it was a miserable place for both these activities. There was no playing field, only a sloping yard fenced off from the inclining ground beyond it, so that balls always disappeared over the fence and into people's gardens where they more often than not got completely lost. At least once a week, after the morning service, the headmaster would read us the school rules, in Welsh and English. I remember the English version of one rule – the only one I was interested in probably: 'Games should be played in such a way that balls do not go over the walls.' Easier said than done!

I hated reading and writing, and letters and words made no sense at all. By now, I know why: I was dyslexic, but there was scant knowledge of that condition when I was in school. Oh no, there was nothing wrong with me apart from my being lazy, useless, lacking in concentration and refusing to listen!

My writing was probably worse than my reading. I was naturally left handed, but was forced to write with my right. In the infant class I had to sit on my left hand when writing because I intuitively picked up my pencil with it. The ruler was a useful tool for teachers in those days too, and not only for drawing straight lines!

I did everything else with my left hand, and have done so throughout my life – when playing cricket, darts, throwing balls, everything apart from writing. Hopefully they are wiser in schools nowadays and don't still believe that writing with your left hand can badly affect your development.

Hating school as I did, it is small wonder that I availed myself of every opportunity to avoid it! And when present I would often ask for permission to go to the toilet, and would also disappear there at the end of every play time. I would shut the door, sit on the seat and prop my feet up against the door so that no one could open it. And that's when the headmaster would come after me with a ruler!

Quite often I would run away from school and down to the town. There, I would have to be careful that I wasn't seen by Sergeant Hughes, as he was always patrolling the square, the police station being nearby. He caught me more than once and marched me back up the hill to the school. Sergeant Hughes lived three doors away from us in Maesafallen, and he knew me well, and that I hated the school, and would escape at the slightest opportunity. When we played silly games on the estate he would come after us wielding his truncheon. I remember his wife as well, she used to sit in her doorway when we played ball in the street, and when the ball went into to her garden amongst the dahlias, she wouldn't let us have it back.

But I found a way to blackmail Jumbo, real name Neville, one of her sons. He was a postman with a round in one of the outlying areas of Corwen. One of the places on his round was Botegir Farm, Llanfihangel, my mother's home. My grandparents lived there and gave him a hearty breakfast every morning.

I told Jumbo that if we didn't get our ball back the next time it went into the garden, there would be no more breakfasts for him at Botegir. I can't remember if the blackmail worked or not.

Dad sold firewood around the houses, and I guess that's where I got the idea to emulate him. When the school bus came to Maesafallen to fetch us in the morning, I would often run off down to Trewyn, the farm across the road, or to the back of the estate to the old railway line, or up the road towards the little cluster of houses called Clawddponcen. My father would have gone to work before the bus came, and Mam would have taken my little sister with her to Plas Isa where she worked as a cleaner, leaving me to my own devices. I once went to Trewyn, placed bricks under the chicken coop and sawed off all the legs to make kindling sticks which I sold for a penny a bundle.

By the side of the old railway line were pieces of fencing, wood that had been creosoted, excellent material for firewood. I would chop them up and make them into bundles and sell them. I was about seven years old at the time, but wise or crafty enough to sell them to old people who didn't ask questions.

When she reached the age of five my sister travelled to school on the bus as well, but she was warned not to tell Mam when I went on the dodge.

I spent every holiday in Botegir with my Taid and Nain. I loved it there, and when I was about nine, Taid taught me how to deliver a lamb. But he would often get cross with me because I did everything counter to him on account of me being left handed of course.

By the time I was eleven the 11+ had come to an end, so off I went to the secondary school, Ysgol y Berwyn, in Bala. Corwen children had a choice of schools – Ysgol Dinas Brân, Llangollen, Ysgol Brynhyfryd, Ruthin or Bala. Since the majority went to Bala, including my friends Barry Williams and David Hughes, that's where I went as well, and stayed there for two months, hating the place as much as I had hated Corwen School.

I suffered from chilblains on my ears; they were very sore and often bled a lot. The geography teacher, as he was walking around the class to check that everyone was working, would slap me on the ear as he went past, not very hard but every touch was like the stab of a knife. One day I threatened to hit him if he did it again.

A week or two later, as he went past my desk, having no doubt forgotten the threat, he gave me a gentle slap on my ear. But I hadn't forgotten! I called out 'Sir' and when he turned around I hit him in the face.

Then I dashed out of the classroom and out of the school and fled into town until it was time to go home. And that was the last time I went to that school. I would go on the school bus to Corwen with the rest of the children and would then go with 'Wil Llaeth,' or 'Bill the Milk' as they used to call him, on his round – to Carrog and Llidiart y Parc, and around Corwen and Cynwyd. He paid me sixpence a week for my help, knowing at the same time that I should be in school. But he deemed it better for me to be with him than wandering about on my own and getting into trouble.

The milk round lasted until lunchtime and then I spent the afternoon helping to wash the bottles. Mam and Dad thought I was in school.

Things weren't too happy at home. My brother Arwyn was the centre of attention there because he was often poorly having only half a stomach and having to go to hospital often for major operations. My dad had his own business but if it rained he would go to the pub with his mates while my mother worked at Plas Isa.

Dad's friends were a bad lot and he often got drunk with them. Saturday nights in Corwen in the 1960s were like scenes from the Wild West. Ieuan Owen, Arthur Wyn and Arthur Davenport were three of his mates. Davenport's wife, Dilys, used to come out of her house to call her children on the estate and you could hear her from Corwen a mile away across the river. Mam would be extremely cross with Dad when he came home drunk on Saturday nights, and things were no better on Sunday, Dad suffering with a hangover and behaving like a bear with a sore head, and Mam angry with him. I would go out of the house at eight in the morning every Sunday and would not return until about eight at night for fear of getting a beating as my parents were in such a foul mood.

During this time, soon after I'd landed a punch in the geography teacher's face in Ysgol y Berwyn, Dad got work on a farm in the Vale of Clwyd and he and Mam decided to move there, and I would never have to worry about the school in Bala again. Mam thought that a fresh start in a new place, far away from Dad's old mates would also give their marriage a new beginning. But, unfortunately, this was not to be. Dad didn't change. Thank goodness, my married life with Susan has been so different to my parents.

iii

Everyone calls me Sue, everyone except Yogi. To him I'm Susan, and he never calls me anything else.

We'd had a wonderful holiday, just the four of us, me and Yogi and the children, eleven-year-old Ilan and Teleri who was nine.

We flew from Manchester to the Caribbean and spent a fortnight there, aboard ship, sailing the seas and calling at several places of interest. A whole fortnight in the sun.

Little did we know that that sun would set so dramatically on our lives.

The previous year, 2006, the four of us went to New York to celebrate my 40th birthday. Yogi would be 50 the following year, so we were keen to do something special to celebrate that as well. Because Teleri had mentioned more than once that she'd love to have a holiday on board ship, the cruise in the Caribbean was that something special. To realise our dream we had to go during the cruising season, weeks before Yogi's actual birthday.

We arrived home on the Wednesday before the Saturday when the last match of the season would be played, a rearranged fixture against Nant Conwy, a match that had been postponed because of a fatal accident, and I've often wondered if it should have been played at all. For months that notion went round and round in my head – an accident before the first fixture and another tragic accident during the second game. Irony or fate – or what? By now I can accept that an accident is an accident and that most occur because someone is in the wrong place at the wrong time.

Anyway, we came home on the Wednesday, calling at Tesco's in Ruthin to get some supplies. Being a school's liaison officer with the police, I was working on the Thursday and Friday, and I remember that I was working in Talsarnau School the afternoon before the game.

My father played for Ruthin Rugby Club before I was born, so I'd always been connected with the game. Before the children were born I always used to watch Yogi play in home and away matches – indeed I once won a prize for being the club's most industrious member during the year, carrying out all sorts of odd jobs, including collecting the money.

But I no longer went to the matches, whether home or away. Each Saturday followed the same pattern: Yogi leaving the house through the garage door, me kissing him and saying, 'don't get hurt,' and 'don't bother coming home unless you've won'.

I remember that particular afternoon in every minute detail. Teleri had gone swimming with some of her friends, Ilan was in his bedroom and I was surfing the internet when the phone rang. The caller was Tony Parry, the club chairman, telling me that Yogi had been injured. I knew at once that things were bad. Yogi never got injured. There was never a phone call. Even when he had to have stitches after an injury in Llandudno, there was no phone call. No, it was inconceivable that Yogi should be hurt.

I immediately got in the car and set out to the ground after asking Marian our next-door neighbour to keep an eye on the children. I remember seeing Teleri on her way home as I left the estate.

I recall being on tenterhooks when I found the road blocked by a lorry in Tegid Street. But Steve Wood came out of his house, showed me a path to the rugby ground around the back of the houses, and promised to take care of my car. I also remember trying to get in touch with my parents and dialling the wrong number. Eventually I got hold of them, informed them that Yogi had been injured and asked them to come over as soon as they could.

When I arrived at the ground Yogi was lying on his back with Geraint Fedw Arian holding his head, and I could see that he was in terrible pain. I remember that there were many people there but the place was so quiet you could have heard a pin drop.

Did I feel bitter? Oh yes, and have often done so. Did I become a bitter person? No. At the end of the day bitterness kills no one but the one who harbours it. Goodness knows I had enough reasons to feel bitter. For this to happen to Yogi, Yogi who never got hurt!

It seemed ages before the ambulance arrived, the doctor in the control room having announced that Yogi's injury was not life threatening. If Yogi's injury wasn't life threatening, I don't know what is. I shudder to think what would have happened to him had not Alwyn Ambulance, one of Bala's paramedics been on the spot. And what would have happened to him had not Geraint Fedw Arian held his head rigid for well over half an hour. Ger's actions were remarkable. I can't imagine how he managed to hold Yogi's head still for such a long time. But Yogi's life depended on him doing just that, and that's what he did.

It is strange the things one remembers. I remember noticing his boots and telling him off because of the state they were in. I remember asking him if he was wearing clean underpants. These things seemed important at the time. He never looked after his clothes or his kit before we were married; he just stuffed everything into his bag, often wet, often covered in mud, and wore them the next time before they had even dried out properly. But once we were married, I put my foot down. He had to bring his kit home to be washed after every match.

The helicopter and the ambulance arrived more or less simultaneously and since Yogi was being conveyed to Wrexham Maelor Hospital, Tony and I followed in his car. I remember being driven through Bala High Street and noticing several people standing around, people who had never done a day's work in their lives or raised a finger to help anyone, and telling Tony after picking one of them out: 'Look at him Tony, no good to anyone but he's alive and well. Life isn't fair.' In my mind's eye I could see Yogi in a wheelchair for the rest of his life. And as we drove I kept recalling him saying more than once that he wouldn't want to live if he lost the use of his legs, and sensing that something much worse than that had happened to him.

I had phoned Joyce, Yogi's sister who lived in Corwen, and she came to the hospital but fainted the minute she saw her brother. When she regained consciousness she said she was going to cancel her trip to Las Vegas. She and her husband were to leave the following day to celebrate her husband's 50th birthday. Yogi told her not to be so silly, but to go on the trip and win heaps of money for us all in the casinos. He could talk at that stage.

Then a friend of ours, Annest, arrived from somewhere. Yogi didn't want to see the children. He was in terrible pain with doctors milling around him. Tony and I, Joyce and Annest were sent to an anteroom to await the verdict on Yogi's injuries. Someone somewhere was screaming blue murder and we learnt later that it was a policeman who had been involved in a motorbike accident. But he wasn't badly hurt. He, after all his screaming was going to be alright, while Yogi who was so quiet, was dangerously ill. It was difficult to banish from my mind these kinds of unworthy thoughts.

A nurse came in and said that they were waiting to hear if there was a bed available for him in Walton. 'Walton?' I asked. 'Walton?' That's where they treat head injuries. She quickly corrected herself. 'I meant Gobowen.' she said. But I sensed that she knew more than she was prepared to tell us.

Yogi needed a ventilator to help him breathe. The level of carbon dioxide in his body was too high and could harm his lungs, and even kill him. So a tube was passed through his mouth into his lungs and that meant that he could no longer talk. The nurse told him that Gobowen couldn't treat him in that condition. The staff of the unit said they had never seen such a severe injury and that it was dangerous to move him; nevertheless he would have to go to Walton in Liverpool.

He was taken to the Intensive Care Unit to await his transfer to Liverpool and I was given the use of a small room nearby. I must have fallen asleep sometime during the night, and I awoke suddenly thinking it was all a dream. Then dawn broke and I realised that it was not just a bad dream. It's hard to describe the terrible feeling of disappointment – it was like cold water being poured on my brain.

This became the pattern for the next fortnight, every time I managed to sleep I would wake up thinking that I had dreamt the whole horrible episode. And something else bothered me incessantly. I kept thinking that Yogi could walk 24 hours earlier, that we were still on holiday the previous week. A fortnight ago there was no cloud on our horizon. And now, our whole world was shattered.

I talked with Yogi on Sunday morning. With the pipe inserted in his lungs he couldn't utter a word, but he could hear and understand everything I said. I explained to him what had happened and told him that he'd lost the use of his body from the neck down. Ever since we were married, and indeed before that, we had agreed that we would always be honest with one another, and I knew that there was no point even then in raising false hopes.

He tried to say something, but I couldn't understand him. All he could do was blink. I told him to blink once for a 'yes' and twice for a 'no'. Then I asked him if he wanted to see the children. He blinked once. To make sure that it was what he wanted I repeated the question. 'Do you want to see the children?' One blink again. I had to arrange this in a hurry before he was moved to Walton.

Joyce drove me back to Bala and I bundled some clothes into a bag and got the children ready. While I was in the house Tony Parry phoned. Some newspaper reporter had contacted him about the accident and wanted a photo of Yogi and details about his children. He'd said that if I didn't comply with his request he would get them anyway. That's when I flew off the handle; Yogi was dangerously ill, fighting for his life and all the newspapers cared about was a picture of Yogi and the children's names and ages.

The press and I were in contention for a long time until Hywel Trewyn, who was a reporter with the *Liverpool Daily Post* at that time came on the scene. My dealings with the press have improved a lot since then: Hywel has been enormously helpful and the *Daily Post* has been very supportive of everything we've done to raise money for Yogi's fund.

Off we went to Wrexham, the children and I, my parents following in another car. On the way I told Ilan and Teleri what had happened to their father. To begin with I told them that he wouldn't be able to walk again, and that he would go about in a wheelchair. And then I said that there was a possibility that he wouldn't be able to hug them any more, but not to worry as they would be able to hug him. The children took the news surprisingly well, as children often do when one has dreaded such an ordeal.

Soon afterwards we heard that there was a bed available in Walton, and so, only hours after the scrum had collapsed on that sunny spring afternoon on Maes Gwyniad, Yogi was on his way on that fateful journey to Liverpool.

CHAPTER 2

Facing the Wind

i

MY FIRST RECOLLECTION after being moved from Wrexham to Walton was of a doctor visiting me to see what could be done about my voice. I lay on a special bed, an iron frame across my chest and around my head, screwed to my skull to keep it steady, with an iron circle like a halo above it. Keeping my head perfectly still was paramount, and every other day someone came to tighten the screws as the swelling in my head went down thereby slackening the frame. There was a sort of blanket not unlike a sheep's fleece on my chest and the frame rested on it.

The doctor withdrew the pipe from my throat to see if I could speak, and I remember telling Susan that I loved her, before the hole was closed up again, and it was three and a half months before I could utter another word. I was constantly sedated in order to keep me still and quiet, given an injection in my belly every four hours to relieve the spasms in the stomach muscles, and I had to swallow 18 tablets every day, some to relieve the pain, some to destroy the bacteria in my throat and some to prevent water retention.

I was peg fed – fed through a pipe to my stomach and the only thing I could taste was salt, due to my constant sweating perhaps, but I wasn't allowed to drink anything. It was like being in the middle of a lake with a big thirst but prohibited from drinking any of the water.

There were four other patients on my side of the ward and a bald-headed man came in every night to give me a morphine injection. Although unable to speak, my mind was clear, or so I thought, and I had somehow convinced myself that he intended to kill me. I was terrified of him, and to make matters worse he never came during the day when there were others around, only at night. There was definitely 'something of the night' about him. In fact I imagined at one time that all the doctors in the hospital were hell-bent on killing me.

During this period I was unable to communicate with anyone, not even by blinking, but I was having terrible nightmares, probably due to all the drugs I had to take.

One recurring nightmare was of five of us sitting in a row at a table, with a huge knife like a guillotine swinging back and forth above us. If we fell asleep the knife would cut our heads off, and this happened to a five-year-old boy, and his head kept rolling about on the floor. Some Indians came and took it away and roasted it, and then my children, Ilan and Teleri had to make a coffin for the boy, but they could not fit him in because his head was too big. Ilan took hold of it by the hair and stuffed it between the boy's legs before placing him in the coffin.

Another nightmare which often disturbed me was of a big man from Jamaica coming into my room trying to steal my shoes, and I couldn't for the life of me understand why, because he wore size 14 shoes and mine were only size 10 trainers. As soon as I was able to, I instructed Susan to ask Aron Bodelith and Tony Parry, two of my mates to come to give him a good hiding and also to attack the bald-headed man who wanted to kill me. Ilan, my son, wears size 14 shoes, so maybe that had something to do with my nightmare!

Susan was in Walton all the time I was there and I received countless operations. They had intended opening both the front and back of my neck, but they changed their minds about that. They decided to replace the fifth vertebrae with a metal plate screwed to my backbone and to rebuild the third and fourth vertebrae.

I now realise that no one expected me to survive the journey from Wrexham to Walton, and they most certainly didn't expect me to survive any kind of surgery. But I had to take a chance. A lad from Neath suffered the same injury as myself whilst playing rugby. But he sadly didn't come through the operation, he sank into a coma and died.

I was unaware of Susan's presence at the hospital until the last couple of days before returning to Wrexham. Long months of recuperation lay ahead of me, but at least I was still alive, having survived all the treatments and operations. Maybe my tough upbringing and the struggle I had against the elements had been an excellent preparation for my fight for life when that became necessary.

ii

Two months before Christmas, before I had completed a term at Ysgol y Berwyn, we moved to Rhiwbebyll Ucha, Llangwyfan in the Vale of Clwyd, where Dad had been offered the post of bailiff on a farm that belonged to L E Jones and his sons, Trefor and Elwyn. They lived on another farm, Bryn Lluarth, and they owned a third, Penbryn, which was also in the vicinity.

It was hoped that this move would signal a new beginning for the family, and that getting away from his mates would improve the relationship between my father and mother, but sadly this didn't happen and matters soon deteriorated further.

Rhiwbebyll Ucha was a pig and sheep farm, and the pigs, having cannibalistic inclinations, had to be regularly fed or they would start eating each other! They were not bred on the farm but bought when six weeks old and fattened prior to being sent to the Halal slaughterhouse in nearby Henllan – a slaughterhouse whose owners didn't believe in eating pork, but were perfectly happy to accept money for killing them!

Dad got up at six in the morning to feed the pigs, before going on the Dexter tractor to Bryn Lluarth where he worked all day, coming home about six to feed the pigs again. Both L E Jones' sons also worked on the farm, Trefor driving the lorry and Elwyn milking the cows.

I had to go to Brynhyfryd School since we lived on the Ruthin side of the border between Denbigh and Ruthin. I turned up in my previous school's uniform, the one that Mam had been given a grant to buy. But there was no grant available to buy a second one, and she couldn't afford a new one for me. I looked ridiculous and stood out amongst all the other pupils in the school, and one boy remarked that I looked like Yogi Bear. The letters YYB were on the school logo on the uniform, which stood for Ysgol y Berwyn, but to the lads, it meant Ysgol Yogi Bear (Yogi Bear School). I was only eleven at the time, but the name stuck and I've been Yogi ever since!

The teachers soon realised that I could neither read nor write, and I was placed in a special education class – the 'Double D' class as it was called – 'drwg a dwl', meaning bad and stupid! The arrangement was that students stayed in this class until they had improved sufficiently to move on from there, but it was where I remained for the rest of my schooldays.

From the very outset I was picked on and bullied by two or three lads from Form 3 because I was different, wearing as I did my Ysgol y Berwyn uniform and bringing sandwiches with me to eat at lunchtime because my parents couldn't afford school dinner. They were usually ketchup sandwiches and I would stay in the classroom on my own to eat them.

About two months into my time at the school, I got fed up with the three bullies. They often came into the classroom while I was eating my lunch to poke fun at me. One day when they'd come in, I got up and locked the door, and then I lost it completely. I picked up a chair and struck one of the three – Bryn Jones – with it, breaking his shoulder bone, before turning on the other two boys. When the teachers heard the commotion they rushed over to the classroom to see what was happening and they had to force the door open to get in. There I was, behaving like a madman, mercilessly attacking the boys with the chair. The one that got it across his shoulder had to go to hospital, and I expected to be severely punished for my actions. However, once the teachers had heard my side of the story, I got away without punishment, because I'd been provoked so much – provocation is the word, I believe – and I was left well alone by those three boys, and by everybody else from then on. I had proved that I was not a lad to be taken lightly or played around with!

I didn't take to the new school any more than I did to Ysgol y Berwyn, although things weren't all bad there. Mr Jones, the special needs teacher, was a small man who wore thick black glasses and had scars on his face. He understood children like me, and he explained why I couldn't read or write. Everything in the classroom was through the medium of English which made things more difficult for me, and I was given a new word to learn every week, and I remember one word in particular that I had great difficulty with, the word *because*. It took me weeks to master it.

Another teacher whom I respected was Gary Evans, the sports and physical education teacher. I liked this subject of course, and he was a very good teacher. But I disliked the science teacher – 'Flash Harry' as we called him, who lived in Gellifor, one of the villages we passed through every day on our way to school.

Like many other teachers in those days his main weapon was the blackboard duster which he used as a missile to throw at us, until strict rules were introduced against the use of physical punishment in schools and homes. Another aggressive habit of his was to hit you in the spine with his knuckles. If he were to do that to me now I wouldn't feel a thing!

I decided to take my revenge on him, prepared carefully for the event, and one day, hid a car jack under my coat and took it to school. He always parked his orange and cream Beetle Camper in the same spot facing the wall in the car park, and when there was no one about I jacked up the back axle and placed bricks under it so that the wheels – the wheels that drove the van – were off the ground.

At the end of the school day, I and a chosen few took up our positions behind some trees to watch the ensuing drama. We saw him start the van and put it into reverse to get out of his parking space, but of course, it never moved an inch, despite all his revving! But instead of pausing to think what could be wrong, he put the engine into first gear and as he moved his foot off the clutch, the van inexplicably rolled off the bricks and he went straight into the wall. The trick had worked better than I ever expected.

The other kids were as overjoyed as I was when they saw this, because he was a most unpopular teacher. And he never found out who had played the trick on him.*

The future looked bleak for me in school, and I remained in the special needs class, labelled the 'dunce' class the whole time I was there. So by the time I reached the age of 13, my attendance had become sporadic to say the least, not that it was anything but very patchy prior to that.

We travelled to school on the service bus, the Brynhyfryd children in the back, and the private school boys – those who went to Ruthin School, in the front. We used to taunt them and hurl insults at them because they were snobs, and one day I threw a conker at one of them, and it inadvertently struck the conductor. He was furious and when we arrived in Ruthin he marched me into the school and to the headmaster's office, where I received six strokes with a brush handle, that being the standard punishment whatever the offence. Barely a week went by without my receiving six strokes for something or other, mostly pretty innocent deeds such as climbing up onto the roof to fetch a ball – strictly forbidden of course, only that I was stupid enough to ignore the rules.

I have always been drawn to the land, and during my first years in school I became acquainted with a farmer, Ifor Roberts, who lived in Llety Fawr, Llangynhafal, through which the bus travelled on the way to school. I had soon perfected the art of failing to catch the bus and, later on, of getting off before it reached the school. Because it was a service bus, it made frequent stops, and I began getting off at Llangynhafal. Then I would walk up to Llety Fawr and work on the farm with Ifor Roberts.

He was well known for the quality of his carrots, indeed he was called 'King Carrot', because of them, and because of his red

---

* A few months after the publication of the Welsh version of this book, a stranger called at our house in Bala. He was Flash Harry's brother, lived in south Wales, had read the book and was absolutely delighted with the story!

hair. Every Thursday and Friday during the autumn he took his carrots to sell in the market. And as I did with 'Bill the Milk' in Corwen, I began to help Ifor Roberts with the selling and with other general duties on the farm.

He was a very kind man and I thought the world of him, he was so good to me, but he could get very angry, maybe because of his red hair. There was a very dangerous sow on the farm, especially violent when she had piglets. I used to help Ifor to castrate the piglets, and we'd conduct the operation in the trailer on the yard, and the sow would pound the sides of the trailer trying to get to her brood. As we castrated the piglets one by one, we let them out, but one day, the sow waited for us, and we had to take refuge in the trailer until she got tired and went away.

But the sow had her comeuppance in the end. One day Ifor put two pet lambs in the same field as the sow, and she attacked them and killed both of them. Ifor got very angry and chased her with a pitchfork and killed her, whilst Mrs Roberts shouted at him from the yard, begging him to stop, but he had lost all self-control, and I could well understand how he felt.

I worked on the farm for two years, and then the inevitable happened and my parents learnt of my truancy, but there was nothing they could do to make me improve my attendance at school.

Pigs played an important part in my life, and because there were pigs at home in Rhiwbebyll Ucha and in Penybryn I definitely learnt a few things about them during my youth. They are strange creatures often attacking the weakest in their midst and killing it. Once they develop a taste for blood, they can be very dangerous.

Dad fed them early in the morning at Rhiwbebyll before going to Lluarth where he worked all day returning in the evening to feed the pigs again before retiring to the house. He was very strong in those days, and could easily carry a hundredweight of pig feed on his back into the sty, and I thought that I could do the same. Into the sty I went carrying the bag across my shoulders, and I immediately fell flat on my face. The pigs, smelling food rushed towards me and attacked me there and then. I was covered in blood and dirt, and was screaming bloody murder. Fortunately Mam heard my cries for help and managed to drag me to safety, and then hosed me down before I went into the house!

Very soon though, I had to feed the pigs myself in the evenings because Dad resorted to his old habits, calling at the Golden Lion in Llandyrnog on his way from work, and coming home drunk two or three times a week.

During this time, apart from working for Ifor Roberts, I also went to other farms to offer a helping hand and to earn some pocket money. One day I saw a bicycle in the window of the Burgess store in Denbigh, a sleek silver Raleigh and I set my heart on buying it. I had been saving my money for a while, and had £70 stacked away, but the bike cost more than that. The shop promised to keep it for me for three weeks, and when Ifor Roberts offered to pay the balance and take it out of my wages I decided to buy it. My money was in a drawer in my bedroom but when I went to fetch it, it had gone, my father had stolen it for beer money and I was devastated. I never forgave him for that, but I got the bike after all, thanks to Ifor.

In spite of all efforts made by the school and the authority – letters to my parents that came via my sister and visits by the appropriate officer – my attendance continued to be sporadic and my week soon developed into some sort of a pattern. I never missed school on Wednesdays, because it was the day when we had sports and physical education, the only subject I enjoyed and that with a teacher I respected. On Thursdays and Fridays I would go to the market and earn some money helping farmers to unload and load their stock. Then, on Friday nights I would catch a bus to Llanfihangel and stay the weekend with my grandparents, Nain and Taid at Botegir. There Taid, having put me on the bus on Monday mornings, was confident that I would reach school safely, but it was false confidence. He had no way of guaranteeing that I'd get there, and of course, more often than not I never did. I would be off the bus long before it reached Ruthin.

Botegir was my haven and my heaven. There was a Land Rover and a tractor there, and I had learnt to drive both of them long before the age of obtaining a licence to do so. One summer, Taid put me on the tractor to work in the hayfield, but I was too small to reach the clutch and the brake, so what he did was set me up on the tractor, jump off and let me go, circling the field until he returned at dinner time! This was before health and safety became an issue, and before a fatal accident occurred on the farm.

I remember two farm hands in Botegir, Haydn, who was seven years older than me, and Bob Jones, a little older, unmarried and living with his parents in Llanfihangel. He owned a BSA motorbike, and he would let me ride on the bike with him to the top of the mountain, and then I'd run back down to Botegir, whilst he went on home.

Sadly, soon after I got to know him, tragedy struck. One day, whilst Bob Jones was cutting thistles on a steep slope, his David Brown tractor overturned and killed him instantly. The accident affected Taid badly, and his hair turned white almost over night. A safety inspector came to the farm to try to find out what had happened. There was no safety cab on the tractor and, when it overturned, Bob Jones had apparently tried to jump clear, but the tractor toppled over and pinned him underneath. I helped to clear the mess and to obliterate all signs of the accident, but it had a lasting effect on Taid whose attitude towards Haydn and I changed after that, especially when using the tractor. Bob Jones was only 31 when he was killed.

My younger sister Angela was born when we lived at Rhiwbebyll Ucha, and so there were four of us: myself, Joyce, Arwyn, the weak one, and Angela. But moving from Corwen had no positive effect on Mam and Dad's relationship, and things gradually worsened. Whenever Dad came home after a bout of drinking, he had no self-control, and was often violent. One Sunday afternoon, he came home drunk and hit Mam in my presence. I hit him back as hard as I could until he fell over the sofa. Then, I locked myself in the bathroom, climbed out of the window, went on my bike to Botegir and never returned home after that.

Botegir Farm was owned by a Mr Glasebrook, a very wealthy man, who owned many farms in the Vale of Clwyd, and near Mold. He told me that I would receive full wages if I stayed with Nain and Taid. It was a very big farm comprising of 1,200 acres of land, with over 1,700 sheep, and Taid was the bailiff. I had, of course, unofficially left school some time before this!

Mam and Dad stayed together for another six months before separating, then Dad went to work for a man called Tom Parry in Dregoch Farm, between Llandyrnog and Bodfari, and Mam with her three children, moved into a house in Aberweeler, Bodfari owned by Glasebrook. Glasebrook had many properties where his workers could live rent-free, and she got the house on the same terms because I worked for him, personally receiving £5 of my wages whilst the rest went to Mam. My parents were eventually divorced but my mother never received a penny from my father to help her with raising the children. I had been receiving a little pay from Taid since I was 13, and most of that then would also go to Mam. After she moved to Aberweeler she found part-time work as a cleaner at the Downing Arms in Bodfari, at Llewenni Hall, and in the local shop.

Glasebrook used to visit Botegir twice a year, once in the grouse season, and once in the fishing season. He had made his money in the cotton industry during the war. The estate manager was William Shaw, and he would come to Botegir once a month to pay our wages. He would also phone Taid every Monday morning to discuss the work that needed doing.

During one visit he brought national insurance forms with him for me to sign, and after doing so without knowing properly what I was signing, I was told that I would be in the army within a week because that is what I had agreed to. He was only pulling my leg, but I believed him and went for some time in fear for my life!

I remained at Botegir until I was 17, hardly going anywhere especially after dark because I had no means of transport except for my bicycle. But when I reached 17 years of age, things changed dramatically.

This was the period when I went to Llysfasi and also passed my driving test. It was Taid and William Shaw who suggested that I should go to the agricultural college on the outskirts of Ruthin. I went by bus to town, and then in a taxi from there to the college, where I only remained for two months, hating it as much as I had hated school. Obviously, I just wasn't cut out for either school or college. At Llysfasi I failed to see the point of what was taught to us because most of it was paperwork, and the practical side of farming played a very small part in the teaching, and, being dyslexic, I was naturally hopeless with paperwork.

But I had good friends there and we had a lot of fun, playing pranks and tricks on each other. There was an English lad in the gang, Jeremy Stephens, who worked on a large dairy farm near Wrexham. He knew the lot! You couldn't tell him a thing that he didn't already know, and he would always come nosing around when we were feeding the pigs. Yes, pigs again. I've never been able to avoid them!

The Llysfasi boar was huge, and had two rings in his nose. But he was a fairly docile creature, most of the time. In spite of his boasting, Jeremy, working as he did on a dairy farm, knew nothing about pigs and one day we wound him up by showing him the difference between the pigs that grazed the land peacefully, and the boar, who looked very wild, which was why, we informed him, he had two rings in his nose.

We succeeded in locking poor Jeremy in the sty with the boar, and he was terrified, cowering in the corner and screaming bloody murder. He couldn't get out because the boar was calmly standing by the door. He had a terrible fright that day, but it did him no harm. He was a snob, who regarded us as country bumpkins, our wellingtons covered in muck whilst his were always clean. But he was much more agreeable after his experience in the pigsty.

During my two months in Llysfasi I passed my driving test,

and there was no holding me back after that. I bought a second hand Ford Escort in Huw Goronwy's sale in Rhuddlan, a blue car with a green stripe. Huw Goronwy knew Taid well, and he had assured me that it would be a good car. Every Friday night, after I passed my test, I would drive down to Bodfari to take Mam to the shop, and then I'd hurry to get her home so that I could go to the Crown at Llanfihangel to play darts.

Nain, by the way, didn't adapt well to progress and when Botegir was connected to the water and electricity services, and this happened when I was about nine, she bought a new washing machine, but she never used it, and I'd still have to handle the wooden dolly in the big tub when helping her with the washing. She also taught me to iron, with the old iron that she would heat on top of the Aga in the kitchen. When she acquired an electric iron, she would still use the old one, and I'd use the new one.

Another innovation that came to the house at that time was the television set. Taid went to Corwen to Astley's shop to buy one, and its introduction made a huge difference to life on the farm. Every Saturday without fail, Taid and Nain would go down to Cerrigydrudion, Nain to do the shopping, and Taid to play dominoes with his friends in the Queens. But they would have to be back by four so that Nain could watch the wrestling! Yes, she got used to the television far quicker than the washing machine and the iron.

Without a doubt, earning my driver's licence and buying a car was a landmark that stood out in my life. I felt as though I'd been set free, as though the wind that had been blowing in my face was now behind me. And of course, having a car was a big help for a young rural boy who wanted to find a girlfriend. This, of course, was many years before I met Susan, or Sue as she is known to everyone except me.

iii

By the time I arrived back in Wrexham with the children, a tube had been inserted in Yogi's mouth and he had been given drugs to calm him and to ease the pain; nevertheless he was conscious of what was happening around him, and that I was there. They had placed a collar round his neck and it was so important for him to keep absolutely still that he remained in his rugby kit which, by now, was in tatters.

Teleri was only nine at the time and she had a terrible shock when she saw her father. She became hysterical, refusing to kiss him and running out of the room without saying a word to him. Ilan, on the other hand, being two years older, although visibly shaken, nevertheless stood by the bed and talked to Yogi as if nothing had happened.

I rushed out to comfort Teleri, upset as I was, and said one of those things that one unthinkingly says, in the heat of the moment. 'If there was a God, he would never have let this happen.' I, who had taught a class of eight to twelve-year-old children in Tegid Chapel's Sunday school!

Teleri looked at me askance: 'Why do you say that, Mam. Isn't there a God then?'

'Of course there is,' I said. 'Of course there is a God, it was only something said without thinking. God will look after us.' And my prayer just then was that Yogi would pull through, for all our sakes because we loved him, yes, but especially for Teleri's sake. Having to live with the memory that the last thing she had done with her father was refusing to kiss him would be a terrible cross for her to bear for the rest of her life.

Mam and Dad also came to see Yogi, having followed us in their car in order to take the children home so that I could stay in Wrexham. Dad was too upset to stay for more than a minute or two. Mam was better. Perhaps women find it easier to show emotion. Later that afternoon Yogi was transferred to Liverpool, to the famous Walton Hospital. A doctor and a nurse travelled with him in the ambulance, because every movement, every bump in the road was a threat to his life. I followed, with Joyce, Yogi's sister and her husband, and although it seemed to be the longest journey of my life, I can't remember a thing about it, not even which tunnel we went through, the old or the new. Or did we go via Runcorn Bridge? I have no idea whatsoever.

The ambulance was driven at a gentle speed as the journey had to be as smooth as possible, but we didn't attempt to follow it. Its lights flashed all the way from Wrexham to Liverpool, but there was no police escort.

Walton Hospital is in Fazacerley and after we arrived I waited to see the doctor. Yogi was placed in the Intensive Care Unit, a large C-shaped ward with eight beds, and he was given a bed at the far end on the left, opposite the door. All the patients were seriously ill of course and each one had a personal nurse.

My best friends know that I love my food but I didn't eat a morsel from the time of the accident on Saturday till Thursday night. I had never before suffered such a trauma, unable to eat and somehow surviving on coffee and water.

There were very strict rules for visiting the unit, no one was allowed in between two and four o'clock in the afternoon and after ten at night until the following morning. I was the first one at the door every morning and the last one to leave every night. I was given one of the four or five rooms at the hospital allocated to the families of severely ill patients, and many of my friends came to keep me company in the afternoons. It was a great comfort to know that the children were with Mam and Dad. They stayed in Bala for six whole weeks, bless them, Dad going home to Caernarfon every so often to pick up the post and check that everything was in order there, whilst I stayed at the hospital to be on hand if I was needed. Yogi was kept there from the Sunday until a week Tuesday.

He was heavily sedated to keep him still, and he was put on traction with weights to try to move the bones. I told them that Yogi had a very strong neck and that they could use heavier weights if they thought it would help, and this they did. They hoped to move the bones before surgery, but they failed.

He was operated on on the Thursday, a massive operation that took hours and hours. Neil Baxter, the surgeon, came to tell me what they intended to do, and that there was only a hair's breadth between success and failure. He said that he used to play rugby and I told him that I thought it was a stupid game.

It was quite an emotional meeting; I was upset and he also had tears in his eyes. I meant what I said at the time but found it hard because Ilan is also a keen rugby player. I know that he's been influenced by his father and of course I don't want to stop him playing, I just want to be there for him, to support him and every time he goes off to play, I say what I always said to his father: 'Don't get hurt.' Rugby is everything to Ilan, it's in his blood like his father before him.

During that terrible time in Walton, Berwyn school's U-12 team were scheduled to play Nant Conwy youth team. Nant Conwy! Of all the teams in north Wales it had to be Nant Conwy. I just couldn't face the fact that Ilan was going to play against them. I phoned Andrew Roberts, the teacher involved, and told him of my feelings. I asked him to consider postponing the game but that I didn't want Ilan to know that I had been in touch with him. Some of the youngsters were making threatening noises – talking about getting their revenge against Nant Conwy, and that isn't really the spirit of the game. But Yogi's accident was fresh in everybody's minds just then.

Neil Baxter talked me through the intricacies of Yogi's operation; they would start at the front, and then the back, and there was a strong possibility that he wouldn't survive the surgery. Before all operations, the patient has to sign a consent form, but this was impossible in Yogi's case. Alternatively, the next of kin has to sign, and that was me. I had an impossible decision to make: if I signed and Yogi died in the theatre, I would forever blame myself, as would others perhaps for my agreeing to such a dangerous operation. If he survived and was paralysed for the rest of his life, he could blame me for not letting him die, or reproach me on bad days, and I knew that there would be plenty of those, although it was not in his nature to reproach anyone.

I voiced my dilemma to the consultant and told him that I would sign if I had to – one would do anything for a loved one – but he agreed to relieve me of my responsibility and arranged for two doctors to sign instead of me. The hospital staff were ready to do anything in their power to help us.

Several of his friends came to see him before the fateful day, they would sit with me by his bed and I would talk incessantly to Yogi: 'You've got to fight this. You've got two children. You've got to fight this for their sakes. But remember if you can't I won't be mad with you.' But Yogi was unconscious and couldn't hear me. And yet…!

I was also trying to force myself to concentrate and focus his unconscious mind on the good times we'd had together. Yet it was the bad times and the quarrelling that seemed to fill my mind, although such episodes were few and far between, and I had plenty of time to think.

Some of my friends came to support me and keep me company during the operation. It was a very tense and worrying time that seemed to go on for ever, but eventually came the good news, the complications were by no means over, nor ever likely to be, but Yogi had pulled through safely. I went into the kitchen and stuffed myself with all the food that was there, I ate as if I'd never seen food before. I can't explain why I couldn't eat after the accident. Heartbreak I suppose: the strongest of us reduced to this. Yogi, the one who solved all our problems, who surmounted every crisis laid low in a few fateful seconds. As a policewoman and liaison officer I am well used to dealing with other people's problems, but Yogi was the one who dealt with any family crisis, always strong and wise and positive.

After the operation Eleri Wenallt taped some messages from the children; Teleri talking nonstop and Ilan butting in from time to time with a few comments and observations. So different from the visit to Wrexham.

Several of Yogi's friends came to Liverpool to visit him between the Sunday and the Thursday night. But there were very strict visiting rules for the Intensive Care Unit: a maximum of two visitors at the bedside at any one time, and an insistence on strict hand-washing routines. As a family we had become familiar with the hand-washing routine on board ship, and when the holiday ended we all said what a blessing it was not having to do it any longer! Little did we know that it would become a ritual in our lives for the next year and a half.

In the days following the operation I have never seen so many men break down and cry. They came in smiling and in high spirits and left sobbing, overwhelmed by the shock of seeing him as he was. Many just came once, others, Aron Bodelith, Tony Parry (TP) the club chairman, and our next-door neighbours', Marian and Alan, came on a regular basis. So did his sister Joyce until at Yogi's insistence she and her husband went reluctantly on holiday, telephoning me every day while she was away.

When Yogi regained consciousness after his long ordeal he had lost his voice, but Aron could understand him, realising very quickly that by standing at a distance he could read his lips when he struggled to try to say something. TP, on the other hand, insisted on getting close to him and putting his ear to his mouth, consequently he couldn't understand a thing.

For three and a half months Yogi couldn't utter a word and during that time TP tried his best to understand him, and he kept on going close to him rather than keeping his distance and reading his lips. And then when his voice came back, I suggested that he play a little trick on TP and pretend that he still couldn't talk. When TP came to see him Yogi opened and closed his mouth like a frog, TP came nearer and nearer as before and when he was right up in his face Yogi called 'Boo!' and TP nearly jumped out of his skin. Silly little games and tricks like this were a source of great comfort at the time.

Yogi now had a frame around his head and a halo-like circle above his head. He had also had a tracheotomy (trachy), so when the children came to see him we had to warn them beforehand about the way he looked. I prayed that Teleri wouldn't rush out this time. I described the ward to them and warned them about how their father would look to them, and cautioned Teleri to keep her eyes on him and not look at anyone else. But I need not have worried, she was fine and she insisted on kissing him, so that Ilan and I had quite a job to lift her above all the frames and wires that surrounded him. Teleri was a completely different person and was upset that she had to leave her father and go home.

Yogi insisted that he could feel the children pressing his hand, and when he returned to Wrexham Ilan also insisted that he'd seen his father's hand move. I also perceived a slight movement and, for a second, I thought that there was hope. But they were only muscle movements or spasms, and he has a pump in his stomach to control them.

At the beginning the spasms were really bad and frequent. One of the nurses who looked after him later on in the Southport Hospital was a tiny Philippino, no more than four feet tall. One day when he was sitting in his chair and she was standing between his legs to treat him, he had one of these spasms, trapping her between his legs so that she couldn't move an inch. It was a serious incident at the time, but became a great source of amusement and leg pulling afterwards.

When they decided to move Yogi back to Wrexham I was only given half an hour's notice. Gethin Jones – Gethin Caerau had come to see me and we were sitting on the wall outside talking. I saw Sister Mary running towards us and for a second I was terrified thinking something terrible had happened, but she was coming to tell us that Yogi was being moved to Wrexham within the half hour.

My immediate problem was that I had no car in Walton; I had arranged for someone to drive it home as cars were sometimes vandalised in the hospital car park. Gethin offered to take me, so I packed my things as quickly as I could and we were soon on our way in the minibus to the park and ride where Gethin had his car. But he hadn't come in the car but in his pick-up and that is how I arrived in Wrexham. Once at the hospital I immediately rushed up to the unit, only to find that Yogi wasn't there. I rushed back down again, but there was no sign of him. Our paths must have crossed while he was in the lift and I was on the stairs. Little things can cause no end of worry and panic at a time of stress.

Our time in Walton was over and it felt like a lifetime. But we forged many good friendships there with people in different circumstances to ours, but similar as well. We were all in a state of emergency and our different stressful situations brought us all closer together. Oddly enough everyone thought that Yogi was a famous rugby player – I suppose it was because he was a Welshman, and they'd mistaken the words 'well known' for 'famous'.

Yogi's last words to me before he lost his voice for months were: 'I love you,' and I could count on the fingers of one hand how often he'd said that in the whole 19 years of our marriage. I would often tease him about it and he would always say: 'Well if I didn't love you I would have left you ages ago.' But to hear the words in that hospital, in such tragic circumstances, meant more to me than anything else in the whole wide world.

CHAPTER 3

Tackle Area

i

A FORTNIGHT AFTER the accident I was on my way back to Wrexham to spend a miserable period in the Intensive Care Unit. It was a terrible journey because I refused to take painkillers as they were giving me hallucinations, so every pothole and roughness in the road was agonising, and lying flat on your back in a fast-moving ambulance is not an ideal way of travelling even for a fit person.

I remained on my back for many weeks after that, with a frame surrounding me whilst six nurses came regularly at two-hour intervals, day and night, to change my position in bed, giving me what they called 'a log roll'. Two at my head, two at my feet and one at each side.

It is more than likely that this constant turning saved me from developing thrombosis; it certainly helped to avoid my having bed sores, and they are terrible things. I suffered from one or two for a short time but nothing compared to one patient I saw in Southport who had been bedridden for nine months and was covered with sores. I was lucky in that respect.

Because I was lying on my back I could see nothing except the ceiling. It was my whole world until two mirrors were strategically placed so that I could observe the entire ward and recognise those who were coming to visit me before they arrived at my bedside. I then tried talking to them and failed, and that made me miserable. I was rather confused at times and misunderstood some situations. One day I noticed that the three other beds in the unit were vacant, and I immediately assumed that the occupants were all dead and that I was the only one left alive.

As a result of lying on my back, fluid gathered in my lungs and it had to be drained at regular intervals. Rachel, the head of physiotherapy, often brought students with her to help her. I wasn't taking painkillers at this time and as a result I had trouble getting to sleep, slumbering all the time but never sleeping properly.

But one of the night nurses had a brilliant idea. Huw Dylan had brought me a bottle of Southern Comfort, and the nurse froze the liquid into cubes and then rubbed my lips with two or three of the cubes every night, and this helped me to relax and fall asleep.

During my time back in Wrexham I developed my own sign language so that I could communicate with others – pulling my tongue out meant yes, closing my eyes – no, and a wink meant that I was fine.

One of the worst aspects of my period in Wrexham was that I had plenty of time to think and to recollect what had happened, and to wonder what would come next. I felt depressed at times, although some things helped me forget such as Bryn Defaity coming to see me straight from work on the farm with his boots and clothes covered in sheep dung, leaving a smelly trail behind him along the ward.

I was given many injections in my stomach every day against the spasms and Bryn asked one of the nurses if he could have some of the syringes that they used in order to inject his sheep!

I knew that I would not be staying in Wrexham but would be transferred to Southport as soon as a bed became available for me there, although the wait could be a long one.

After about a month in hospital three of the Southport staff came to see me: Mr Soni, the medical consultant; Clive Glass, the psychologist and Jenny Bingley, head of nursing. They came to assess my mental state and I was asked many questions which I naturally had great difficulty in answering. Their objective was to discover my attitude towards my injury and towards life in general. Did I want to live? Was I depressed? What did

I envisage happening to the children? Did I want to see them growing and developing? These and many other questions.

Mr Soni then pricked me with a pin, all over my body to see where I had feeling and which parts of the body were numb. Then he told me that he was willing to accept me as a patient in Southport if I was determined to try to get well and was positive in my attitude. He added that I would have to have a voice box installed in order to be able to speak, that I would never be mouth-fed again and that I would never be able to move my head. By now I can speak without a voice box, I can eat and I can move my head!

The three left saying that it could be November before there was a vacancy for me at Southport, but a fortnight later the call came to say that there was a bed available and I was to be moved the next day. The date was 6 June, and I had to face another uncomfortable journey lying on my back and in great pain. Yes, it was a miserable journey but not without its adventure.

About halfway to Southport the ventilator stopped working properly, the battery was low because, believe it or not, it hadn't been charged before we set out. So speed was essential and we sped along highways and byways as the driver sought out the shortest route, and miraculously we arrived at the hospital before I collapsed. A very stressful and painful journey indeed! Little did I realise it at the time, but this was the hospital where I was to spend the next year and a half of my life.

ii

Cars and alcohol don't mix, but mix them I did when I was young! I passed my driving test on my first attempt, in the Land Rover, in Bala, which was considered an ideal place as it was a town without roundabouts. Taid came with me as the experienced driver. The Land Rover didn't have a very good lock and I drove over the pavement as I turned off the main street into Tegid Street and was convinced that I had failed.

An important part of the test was the emergency stop, and I

had been told by someone that the tester would require me to do one of those on the stretch of road between Bala and Llanfor. I was therefore keeping one eye on him and when I saw him lift his file to strike the window in front of him, I hit the breaks hard and he nearly went flying through the windscreen. When I finished the test and returned to where I'd started, Taid was standing on the pavement waiting for me, and I got out of the Land Rover and told him that I had failed. But the man called me back and told me that I had passed, which was something of a miracle!

I had started playing football for Cerrigydrudion when I was 16 years old. Passing my test and buying myself a Ford Escort gave me the freedom that I had longed for. Not that I was entirely tied down before that either as I used to go on my bike to Cerrig to train, and then to the Saracens Hotel and down to the Goat Hotel in Maerdy and home through Betws Gwerful Goch, a round trip of about 15 miles.

Cerrig played in the Conwy League, Second Tier, North Wales, against teams such as Penmachno, Conwy, Llanrwst, Llandudno and Mochdre and it was a good league. Cerrig didn't have a very good team to start off with but it developed quite soon and we won the league four or five times. I was centre forward.

During the 1980s I won quite a few trophies and cups while playing football – such as the trophy for being the highest scorer for Cerrig in 1979/80, coming second in the league the same year and winning the Challenge Cup, winning the Jack Owen Cup in 1980 and the Tucker trophy in the Conwy League in 1982/83. I won most of them with Cerrig, but a few with Cynwyd and Llandrillo's five- and seven-a-side teams as well. And, of course, the Bragdy Cup in Bala was very important even after I started playing rugby, we won in 1992 and 1995 and came second in 1994.

The Ford Escort came in handy to take Mam shopping, to go to football training, to go to play darts, and to go drinking! It was much better than the bike.

Soon my life developed a regular pattern: training two nights a week, darts one night, taking Mam shopping on another night, then during the summer, two nights playing football in the Summer League with every night ending in the Crown in Llanfihangel, the Glanllyn in Clawddnewydd, the Goat in Maerdy, or the Saracens in Cerrig. The Saracens is a hotel on the A5 in Cerrigydrudion, and there we had the use of a little room called the snug, a haven for underage drinkers! There was a large dancing hall in the hotel as well and that's where the owner at the time kept his vintage car. His wife ran the hotel.

It was to the Crown in Llanfihangel that I went most often to play darts and very soon I was a member of the team which played in the Ruthin and District League. Darts night was Friday and I would rush there after taking Mam shopping. I won many trophies with the darts as well as the football, in 1977, 1979 and 1980. We came second in the league during these years, but in 1987 we won.

I had no friends I could call my own until I started playing football. Older people who played dominos with Taid in the Queens and his acquaintances were also my acquaintances: Moi Em, Wil Yates and Jac Foty Llechwedd. The ones who played darts in the Crown were older than me as well – amongst them were Gwil Llwyn and Trebor Edwards – and as I had left school almost before starting there I didn't have any friends amongst the former pupils. Things changed when I seriously started playing football.

I was centre forward, and when I started playing some of the Cerrig lads were nearing the end of their careers – Huw Doctor, Hefin Penbryn and Dei Sgŵl. The team was run by Dei Rich, who kept a butcher's shop in Cerrig, and the team played on a very poor pitch until the firm which built the dam at Llyn Brenig came to the rescue, and designed a new pitch, a fact that has been recorded in stone in the ground.

Two brothers from Penmachno played for two of the Conwy League teams, Martin Lloyd in goal for Llanrwst and Ken Lloyd as centre half for Penmachno. These two were very aggressive, and would often be sent off. Although they were brothers they couldn't play in the same team as they kept arguing with each other all the time!

In the first game that I played against Llanrwst, Martin Lloyd was in goal and I scored three goals against him, and he was fuming. Later on he came to play for Cerrig and he was a good goalkeeper. I played against his brother Ken many times as well, and I remember one game in particular, it was a Cup match against Penmachno and we were awarded a corner kick. I stood on Ken Lloyd's feet and headed the ball into the net. As I walked back to the centre spot I was hit on the back of my neck and when I turned around to see who it was I saw Ken Lloyd's Mam with her umbrella; she had been watching on the touchline and didn't like what she saw!

As a result of going to Bodfari every Friday night to take Mam shopping, and also playing in the Summer League all summer, I got to know the lads in that area, and it was with them, and not Cerrig lads, that I used to go out. We'd go to Rhyl and Prestatyn, and more often than not I would drive but that never stopped me drinking when we went to pubs and dances.

One night in Rhyl, I met a girl from Birmingham, who was staying in a caravan in Prestatyn. I had been drinking all evening, but at the end of the night I took her back in the car to her caravan. I was stopped by a policeman on the way, and he started searching my car, he searched the boot thoroughly and somehow managed to pull the back seat out of its place. He obviously knew what he was looking for, but he wouldn't say what it was and he didn't find anything either.

'You've been drinking,' he said, having probably smelled the alcohol on my breath.

'I had a little shandy,' I said.

He went to his car to fetch the breathalyzer – the old-fashioned bag with the green crystals in it that changed colour if somebody had drunk too much.

To my surprise the crystals stayed green and he had to let me go.

In the early hours of the morning I returned from the caravan and headed home travelling on the coastal road towards Rhyl. In exactly the same place as I was stopped some hours earlier, I was stopped again, but by a different policeman this time. He went through the same routine, searching the car and the boot thoroughly without saying what he was looking for. I had to blow into the bag for him as well and again the crystals remained green.

Yes, I was very lucky, but the experience didn't cure me, in fact it made me worse. I thought I was Jack the lad after that, and thought I could hold my drink, drink as much as I liked and still drive. There was no stopping me; I would go everywhere in the car and would drink without a care in the world – with Bodfari and Caerwys lads, the Summer League lads in the summer and the Cerrig and Conwy Valley League lads in the winter.

Early summer was a busy time in Botegir, the sheep – all 1,700 of them had to be washed, dipped and sheared. We would dip them in the river, digging a huge hole in the bed of the river to deepen it and then reverse an old trailer to the bank and drop the sheep from it into the water. A very old tried and tested way of going about it, but most effective. Then, the shearing would take place for days on end, and after finishing at Botegir I would help out on other farms in the area.

On one farm I met a girl from Penarlâg (Hawarden); she was wrapping wool in the pen, and at the end of the day I took her home to Penarlâg and returned in the early hours of the morning.

After a hard day's work and a late night I was tired and sleepy, but I managed to keep myself awake by opening the window, and finally I turned off the main road from Llanfihangel to Cerrig and onto the narrow private road that led to Botegir.

'I'm fine now and almost home' I said to myself and I must have relaxed and fallen asleep for a few seconds because the next thing I was conscious of was a terrific jerk and bang that woke me up in an instant. A telegraph pole had fallen across the bonnet! I had driven straight into it and it had snapped clean off at the base!

But I knew what to do. I took the pole and chopped it into firewood, then cleared the glass – from the shattered car lamp – without leaving a trace, and then shaved a bit of hair from the bull's neck and rubbed it on the base of the pole, the part that was still sticking out of the ground.

In a day or two some men from BT came to the farm and believed that it was the bull that had collided with the pole and snapped it. Lucky! A new one would have cost me a £100 had they realised that it was my car that had collided with it, and not the poor bull!

Taid somehow got hold of the story and he also knew that I was drinking. But Nain didn't know, or I thought that she didn't. I would chew some extra strong mints before breakfast to hide the fact from Nain, but I think she knew. She herself was dead against alcohol.

Life on the farm followed a regular pattern: in the summer I was out early, and then back to the house mid morning to have a full breakfast and then out again until evening. The hours were regular for most of the year but during the lambing and harvesting seasons they were very long and overtime was unheard of.

When I was 18 I had an argument with Taid, the only argument I ever had with him. I don't remember what caused it, but it was something to do with the sheep with both of us disagreeing vehemently.

'If that's how you feel,' I said, 'then do it yourself.' And for a few days after that I started working at eight in the morning and finishing at five, keeping religiously to those regular hours and refusing to work any later.

It was then that I decided that I'd had enough of farming and wanted to go into the army. I applied and travelled to Wrexham for a medical. I was certain that I would be accepted as they needed many soldiers at that time, especially with all the trouble going on in Ireland.

As I thought, I passed the medical and was accepted. The difficult part then was to break the news to Taid and Nain. I decided that the wisest thing to do would be to tell Nain first. I knew that she got up at half past five every morning, and so one morning I did the same and went into the kitchen. She was sitting by the table with a cup of tea and there was a small bottle of whisky on the table as well. She, who was so much against alcohol, was having a shot of whisky in her tea every morning!

I told her the news, feeling myself to be quite a lad leaving the farm and joining the army, and sounding very determined. But she had no trouble at all in changing my mind. She started reminding me how much she and Taid had done for me and Mam over the years, and where would we be if it wasn't for them! Taid she said was getting old and was relying more and more on me every day.

After what she said, all thoughts of joining the army disappeared. In the game of life, there I was thinking that I was a good centre forward, the most glamorous position on the field, and I had met a centre half who could tackle even harder than I could. I realised that they had been looking after me from the time I was twelve, and now, as they were getting older, it was time for me to repay them for all that care and to stay to look after them.

The next decade, until I was 28 years old, were years of working on the farm, of drinking, of playing football and of chasing girls. And marrying the right one in the end!

iii

I only had coffee and water to sustain me in Walton, but I must admit to smoking rather a lot as well. Travelling back to Wrexham with Gethin, I sprayed myself rather liberally with perfume to disguise the smell of cigarette smoke. When he arrived home Gethin had to explain to his wife Siân how the heavy scent in the pick-up got there! Yogi, of course, knew of my smoking habits, but I didn't want to upset him in the hospital. By the way I have never smoked in the presence of my parents – and I'm over 40 years old!

I shall have to conquer the habit, if only for the children's sakes, but it isn't easy. I managed it once for eight whole days, then there were problems with the company who employed Yogi's carers, and that set me off again.

When Yogi was moved back to Wrexham following his operation in Walton, my daily routine changed as well. That evening I came home with Gethin, went back to Wrexham by midday the following morning and stayed there until eight o'clock

I availed myself at last of the opportunity to establish some sort of pattern to my days which included spending some time with the children. But it was a very tiring and trying time: setting out to Wrexham at eleven in the morning and arriving home at nine in the evening. Then there were people calling and people phoning and I was getting more and more exhausted by the day. I don't know what I would have done had not my parents been there to take care of us all.

In Wrexham, Yogi was in the Intensive Care Unit and I could stay with him all day and all night if I wished. But I stuck to the pattern I had planned for myself except for two days and a night during the Urdd National Eisteddfod week in Carmarthenshire. The Urdd Eisteddfod is purported to be the biggest youth festival in Europe and those who appear at the National do so by a process of elimination in local and county festivals. Teleri had qualified in the harp solo competition for the U-12s and Dorothy Ann Jones (the headteacher of her primary school – Ysgol Bro Tegid), arranged for us to stay the night with relatives of hers at a farm near Carmarthen where the National was held.

Being away from home and so far from Wrexham made me very anxious and I can't say that I enjoyed myself. But I had to make the effort for Teleri's sake. We as a family had made all the arrangements for this event before the accident, and had booked for the four of us to stay at a hotel for the duration of the Eisteddfod – another dream shattered.

Although I spent as much time as possible at Yogi's bedside, I felt utterly useless there. Yogi had some sort of contraption full of air in the pipe fixed around his throat. It was possible to release the air for a few seconds every now and then and that was the only time he could talk. As he still depended on one-to-one nursing, I asked the senior nurse if I could do anything to help, and it was agreed that I could care for him from late afternoon until visiting time. I could wash him and prepare him for visits and that meant the world to me. I didn't find the task easy, but at least I was doing something to help Yogi. At home he was always the one who tended to the children when they were ill, he was the one who cleared up after them, tasks that turned my stomach. Now I had to grit my teeth and get on with it.

The Maelor Hospital in Wrexham didn't have the necessary facilities to nurse patients like Yogi who suffered from spinal injuries. His stay there was only an interim arrangement until a bed became available for him at the Formby and District General Hospital in Southport where there was a specialist unit for such cases. We were given to understand that there could be a six-month wait, but in fact a bed became available in a few weeks. The only other suitable unit was the Orthopaedic Hospital in Gobowen, which would have been much more convenient, being nearer to Bala, but because he needed help with his breathing, they couldn't take him there.

During this period he was often very confused, the result of all the drugs and tablets he was given, and he often got the wrong end of the stick. He lay on his back on a bed in the corner of the ward inside a metal frame, being fed through his stomach many times a day, and unable to see a thing except in the mirror above his head. But he could hear everything.

The physio came to see him one day with an entourage of students. They were there to be taught to recognise the different sounds heard in his lungs through the stethoscope and to learn their names. 'That,' she said to the group, 'is a bronchial sound.' That evening the nurses reported that Yogi was alright, but if I read his lips correctly he told me that he had bronchitis!

There were only four beds in the ward and he could see the other three in the mirror. One day he noticed that the other beds were all empty and he managed to convey to me that evening that the other three had died and he was the sole survivor! There was a simple explanation of course; one patient had been moved to the general ward, another to the High Dependency Unit and the third to another hospital.

We were agreed on one thing, that we would be entirely honest with each other, something we had always adhered to during our married life. But he upset me terribly one day.

After a few weeks I had started to plan our future, and think about the time when Yogi would be allowed home. Our house would have to be adapted to suit his needs or we would have to build a suitable bungalow. I had been looking at a possible site for a bungalow further up our road, and some of Yogi's farmer friends had offered land to build on, and we would have to seek permission from Snowdonia National Park Authority. So many things to think about, and I mentioned all these various options to Yogi.

'There is one other option,' he told me. 'You can put me in a home, and you have my permission to do that.'

I was furious when I heard this. 'Don't you dare say that ever again,' I shouted through my tears. 'That is not an option, never has been, and never will be. And if you say such a thing ever again and think that breaking your neck is a problem, it'll be the least of your problems.'

Yes, things were difficult, hurtful things were said sometimes, but Yogi had to understand that the options were up to me. It must be remembered that what had happened had happened to all of us, it affected the whole family, not just Yogi. And yet he had to suggest that option, in case at some time in the future we would hold it against him. He had offered it hoping that we would make the right choice. And as a family we had made it.

At first it was hard to see how our present home could be adapted to cater for Yogi's needs, mainly because of the lie of the land. But finally, after careful planning, the sloping land became an advantage, something which could not have happened had we lived in the town.

While all these things were happening, life went on, the

children celebrated birthdays, and I started thinking, with Yogi back in Wrexham, that everything that could happen had happened and that nothing else could confront us. But I was so wrong.

The doctor came to see me in Wrexham to explain what could happen to Yogi. He told me that the surgery had been successful and that everything that could be done had been done. There was no danger of Yogi dying directly as a result of his broken neck, but he went on to list the many complications that could kill him: an embolism or clot could cause his death, pneumonia could be fatal, any fever could kill him. Because of the pipe in his throat something could go wrong in a second with fatal results within minutes – and that's why he needed specialist care 24 hours a day. Another rugby player had recently died, not from his injuries but from other causes arising from his injuries. The only comfort is that the older Yogi gets the less likely it is that all these things could happen.

On the first Monday in June my parents went on holiday, a holiday that had been arranged ages ago. They weren't keen to go, wanted to postpone in fact, but I insisted that they went, they badly needed a break. As Yogi was in Wrexham I could change my routine by going straight to the hospital after the children had gone to school and be back by the time they came home. Teleri was still in primary school and Ilan only in his first year in the secondary school.

Mam and Dad left for Lake Garda in Italy and that very night Sister Sarah Anglesey phoned me and I thought that something terrible had happened. But she was phoning to tell me that there was a bed available in Southport and that Yogi would be moved there on the Wednesday.

I immediately panicked, but Yogi insisted that I was not to visit him in Southport on that day. He said that by the time they got him there and got him settled it would be late and he would be exhausted. As usual he was considering others before himself.

And so I took the children with me to say goodbye on the

Tuesday night, and to take presents to the staff to thank them for all they had done during his stay there.

I was very busy on the Wednesday and I entered all the day's activities on my web diary:

> Prepare the bin and put it out for tomorrow's collection – one of Yogi's usual chores.
>
> Cleaned Ilan's school shoes – one of Yogi's usual chores.
>
> Took Teleri to Blaenau Ffestiniog for her harp lesson – one of Yogi's usual chores.
>
> Bill came to mow the lawn, he and Gwyn taking it in turn to do this – one of Yogi's usual chores.
>
> Alan next-door took Ilan out on his bike – one of Yogi's usual chores.
>
> Washed the car – one of Yogi's usual chores.

And all this made me think what on earth was my usual contribution to the household. Obviously not much when Yogi was around! So much had changed with the family's main spring flat on his back in hospital.

On the Thursday I drove alone to Southport, using the M56, joining the M6 and then crossing to the M58 and got completely lost. I found the hospital eventually and that was when I fully realised how Yogi would be for the rest of his life. In Wrexham he was the only one with this type of injury, in Ward 3 in Southport the place was full of patients in wheelchairs, all with varying degrees of injury, but all of them in severe conditions and unable to move. The place was totally depressing.

After being fed for the last two days in Wrexham it was now back to 'nil by mouth' once again. He was tired after the previous day's journey, so I read him an article from the *Denbighshire Free Press* newspaper about a quiz team from the Royal Oak in Corwen raising £100 for Yogi's fund – a fund initiated by the rugby club which was quickly gathering momentum. Then I told him that Ann Carregberfedd had phoned to say that the proceeds from Cerrigydrudion's rugby tag night would also be donated to the fund. On hearing all this Yogi got quite emotional, and couldn't believe that people could be so kind. I had to remind him that no one had a bad word to say about him and that he really was the salt of the earth.

During this time hopes were raised many times only to be dashed again. The picture drawn by the specialist from Southport who had assessed him in Wrexham was a very dark one – he was not to move his head, nor eat, nor speak except though a voice box. But we had our hopes, and some of them were realised.

Unfortunately we weren't told everything. No one sat down with me to explain the situation in depth. I had to ask and ask in order to get any answers. I needed to form a complete picture of our predicament, but they were reluctant to release any information unless it was in response to specific questions. I studied the Internet for any crumbs of information, and other people like Brian Lloyd were doing likewise. Brian told me that there were conditions of 'incomplete' and 'complete' in the context of serious injuries and that I should ask the experts about it. If an injury was 'incomplete', a part of the spine could still work, but if it was 'complete' as in Yogi's case, then there would be no progress whatsoever.

By surfing the web I learnt that there was a hospital in Beijing that offered specialist treatment to patients with severe spinal injuries. I even went so far as to correspond by e-mail with one of their doctors who raised my hopes considerably. But when I'd considered everything as rationally as I could, I knew in my heart of hearts that going to China was not an option. They kept no statistics, and for all I knew, if they'd managed to save one patient, many others could have died undergoing the same treatment. If there were statistics that showed that eight or nine in every ten had improved, it would be a different story. We would have to raise an enormous amount of money to go to China, £20,000 for the treatment alone, plus the expense of the journey. Anyway Yogi would never survive such a journey across the world. So, in spite of the temptation, that dream had to be scrapped. As I said if the treatment was so successful there would be statistics to prove this and the treatment would surely be available nearer home.

And so it was one day at a time in our lives during this period and we still embrace that philosophy to this day. But we are still hopeful. Yogi is willing to try anything, and he is more than willing to be a guinea pig if that benefits someone else.

Of course, there are good days and bad days, and he naturally has bouts of depression from time to time. I sometimes think that the medication administered through his stomach causes him to look on the dark side of things. I remember him telling me after a painful sleepless night: 'they would never let an animal live like this.' But it was the pain talking.

Naturally this kind of talk upsets both myself and the children. Ilan said, 'Don't be upset Mam, things could be much worse, Dad could have died.' Perhaps we worry too much about our children, they often have more strength and good sense than we credit them with. This has been a very difficult time for Ilan and Teleri, but they've pulled through.

'Out of the mouth of babes...'

CHAPTER 4

In the Sin Bin

i

FEAR WAS MY first companion in Southport, in an alien environment and not knowing what was happening. Susan was unable to come with me since her parents had gone on holiday, and the process of moving me from hospital to hospital and subjecting me to all sorts of tests took all day until five o'clock in the afternoon. There were two or three doctors and countless nurses by my bed, constantly prodding and testing and fixing pipes and instruments all around me. I was told nothing and I couldn't ask; Susan's presence would have been a blessing, but that was not possible.

Later on I was informed that one of the tests conducted on me was for MRSA, a precaution because it was present in Wrexham. But the attitude here was the same as in Wrexham, where there were many people milling around and much going on; not one word of explanation was uttered and I had to depend on one-to-one situations in order to glean any information. Then everybody was prepared to talk and explain. As far as I know this situation is the same in every hospital, you have to ask before you are informed, and asking in my position was difficult if not well-nigh impossible.

I was lying flat on my back exactly as I had been in Wrexham and they were finished with me by five. A staff nurse, Margaret Maule, came to sit by my bed and she looked after me for the next two nights. She was quite exceptional, getting me settled by talking to me all night long in a one-to-one situation and telling me about herself. Speaking English was not my strong point, but since I could not utter a word in any language at that time, hearing English being spoken was a great help. It went into my head and hopefully it would come out when I could speak for myself!

In the morning staff nurse Lee Francis came in, and he stayed with me all day for the first two days of my stay there. He also told his story, and the history of the hospital and we became great friends. Susan visited me two or three times a week which wasn't easy for her considering the distance from Bala to Southport, besides the fact that the responsibility for the home rested entirely on her shoulders.

I was fed though a peg in my stomach and had to take a great number of tablets, about 18 a day so I was hardly conscious of where I was during the first fortnight of my stay. But the numbers were gradually decreased as time went by. I became more conscious of what was happening, started to get the feeling back in my stomach and gradually become acquainted with some of the nurses. The worst thing was my inability to speak. When the frame and halo were put around my head I was told they would have to remain there for at least four months. But after less than three months, the specialist Mr Soni came in one day with something resembling a toolbox and, without telling me what he was going to do, he started taking spanners and other instruments from the box and began to unscrew first the halo, then the frame, throwing the parts on the floor. When he had finished he grabbed my hair, held my head up and then let it fall back on the pillow.

'Neck strong enough without a collar,' he said. 'I'll be back in three weeks' time and expect you to be able to move your head.' And with that he went, taking his toolbox and frame parts with him.

He left me there, unable to speak or do anything and with my head feeling as if it weighed a ton. It was so heavy, almost impossible to move, and for a long time I failed. But I had to persevere, to move it up and down and from side to side. I had assured Mr Soni and the others in Wrexham that I was determined to get as well as I could, and it was on that basis that they had accepted me in Southport. I had to keep my promise, and of course I wanted to get well, so I started exercising and gradually, little by little, I managed to move my head slightly to the left, but turning right was almost impossible. When the specialist came back he was very happy with the movement to the left but said that more effort was needed to improve the movement to the right.

During this time also, because the tablets were being reduced, I became better acquainted with the nurses, and more conscious of friends coming to see me, but the frustration was greater because I was unable to converse with them.

Mr Soni returned, took out the pipe I had in my neck and replaced it with another one.

'I'll be back in a fortnight,' he said, 'and I expect to hear you speak.'

That was all. No explanation for anything only a pipe taken out and another put in.

The voice did return, and it was such a joyous feeling. But English came out the wrong way, although I had heard a good deal of the language. I was thinking and talking in Welsh in my head, and endeavouring to get it out in English, and I said some funny things to begin with. But I was fortunate to have heard them all around me speaking English and so had familiarised myself with their accent before I started speaking myself. And I was getting plenty of opportunities to speak Welsh when Susan and other people came to visit me. A car load of Llangwm lads came every six weeks, as well as two or three car loads from Bala. Oh, it was such a nice feeling getting my voice back and I progressed a great deal after that.

The sister in charge of the ward was a big lady called Carol Fairhurst and everyone was scared stiff of her. To see her was enough, she didn't have to say anything, and she only had to call once to make everyone come running. But she was excellent with me, although she often reprimanded me for not shaving. She said that everyone in her ward looked tidy and shaved every day, and I told her that I had never shaved cleanly. What I used to do was refuse to be shaved when she was on duty and shaving on her days off in order to wind her up the wrong way!

But to be fair to her, when the effects of the tablets receded she came to tell me what would happen next. She explained to me what the odd feelings were that I had in my body internally and externally. It is difficult to explain but they were odd sensations. I was completely paralysed from the neck down, and yet I sometimes felt movements in my stomach and in my arms and legs. I couldn't understand what was happening, being able to feel every muscle in my body and yet unable to move. I could also feel pain, but not every pain and that was dangerous because pain is a warning, a signal. When I went to the physio and he put me on a bike to move my legs it was a most unusual sensation seeing my body move and feeling that it didn't belong to me. I could see my joints moving and bending but it made no sense to me. Often at night I couldn't sleep because I was straining myself in an attempt to move my legs, but failing every time. The nurses kept bringing cups of tea and tumblers of water for me and I wanted to grasp them but I couldn't. To put it simply, my body would not respond to the demands made on it by my mind.

In an encyclopaedia in hospital I saw the picture of a skinless body, showing all the muscles and joints, and I think that this picture represents closer than anything else how I sensed my own body, exactly like the body in the picture.

I had a hard time of it with my throat after I had recovered my voice. The first pipe installed for my breathing was seven centimetres in diameter and kept blocking all the time. The trachy, as it was called, had to be changed four or five times a week, sometimes twice a night because I was choking. There were two persons responsible for the ventilator, Dr Watts and Sue Perrie Davies, and they kept trying different pipes, about six in all until my throat bled. So I had terrible pains. A camera was used to investigate and the problem was that everyone's windpipe is different and the trachy that I was given was too long and rubbed against the back of my throat causing it to bleed.

This was a difficult period for me. I had a hard time of it and didn't want to see anyone because my spirits were low. I will say more about my friends who came to see me later, but when anyone came from Bala I didn't have the heart to refuse to see them since they had travelled a long distance to visit me.

Yes, the period when there was trouble with the ventilator was a difficult time for me, and it was made worse because I didn't understand what was going on, and no one tried to explain until Carol Fairhurst, the charge sister came and told me what was happening, describing the functions of various pipes and what the variety of tablets that I took were supposed to do to me.

During this period I suffered terrible spasms and pains and I was given tablets to relieve them, but they didn't work and the pains were so dreadful they made me bounce on the bed. The spasms had the effect of locking my muscles and the pains were like cramp pains, only worse. They were at their worst in August 2007 although I am still getting them. The trouble was that the muscles were closing on the trachy as well and affecting my breathing. The air went in alright but didn't come out, and so the trachy had to be removed in order that the air could be expelled. The spasms would last for three to four hours and, although various tablets were tried, none of them could dull the pain completely. I was lucky that I could fight everything else without taking tablets, but not the spasms.

About this time I was given the choice of eating if I wanted to, rather than being fed through a pipe to my stomach, and I regarded this as an important development. But it wasn't easy! I remember once in Wrexham when Susan was cleaning my teeth before visitors came, she brushed so hard that the toothpaste came out through the pipe. And the same thing happened when they tried to give me ice cream.

After having decided that I would try to eat rather than be fed through the 'peg' in my stomach and promising Carol that I would eat porridge for breakfast every morning, a man came with a pair of pliers and sat on my stomach. Inside my stomach was some contraption similar to a balloon and they inflated it to prevent the peg from coming out. The man burst the balloon with a loud bang and then he tugged at the peg and pulled it out. I had some inkling of what he was doing but once again there was no explanation, and it was an uncomfortable experience.

And so I began to eat porridge, and what a messy event it was to begin with, I was like a little child being fed and the porridge was everywhere. I ate only a spoonful or two at first and then increased the quantity little by little, and eventually I was given small pieces of brown bread so that I could begin to re-learn how to chew. As with speaking, I had to learn slowly, and they told me that I was lucky that I had two languages since learning was easier. I ate porridge for a year and a half, but I never touch it now! By persevering things got better.

It was rather frustrating to see everybody else being allowed to eat whatever took their fancy whilst I had no choice but porridge, porridge, porridge. But I had to keep at it, otherwise the peg would be back in my stomach and I didn't fancy that. Whilst being fed through the peg I could only taste salt. My stomach had shrunk since it hadn't being receiving any food so it had to be gradually stretched again and at least the porridge did the trick.

Then, after about a fortnight or three weeks of nothing but porridge, the dietician came to see me, to tell me how much protein and Vitamin C and various other elements I needed. But I wasn't allowed to choose what I ate, only what she recommended.

Clive Glass the psychiatrist, nicknamed 'Shrink' by me, wanted to come and see me when I felt low, but I didn't want to see him and I always refused. They eventually told Susan.

I felt very low at times, but tried not to show it to anyone, especially when Susan and the children came to visit me. She came two or three times a week and the children on Saturdays. Susan's mother and father, Dick and Morfudd, were very faithful visitors as well, coming regularly. They and Joyce, my sister, were the only members of family who came. One of the hardest things to bear was to see other patients' families visiting, but not my family. My mother and one sister and brother came to see me twice whilst I was in Wrexham, and Mam came twice to Southport during my first six weeks there. That is all. I haven't seen my mother since then, or any other family members except for Joyce. I can't explain why Mam kept her distance; she was unable to accept the facts perhaps, unwilling to face reality and not having the heart to see me as I was. Not one member of my extended family, such as cousins came either. I don't feel bitter and I don't think much about it. But one comes to realise who one's friends are fairly quickly. Joyce has been ever so faithful to me and still comes visiting every fortnight.

I had seen people who were in the same boat as me in hospital, indeed some who were even worse than I was. When I heard the details of what had happened to some of them, I could believe that life for me wasn't too bad after all. And visits from friends made up for the lack of family visits, between ten and 15 visitors every week, never less than ten unless I had sent a message through Susan that I didn't want to see anyone, and that happened about three times. The hospital had never witnessed such a deluge of visitors, and the staff had no idea either what kind of life I lived when I started telling them about farming. And their lives also were completely different to what I had imagined.

Joyce and Helen were two of the nurses who worked nights and they often came to see me. Helen was Welsh, came from Llangefni and lived after her marriage in Southport. It was nice to have someone to speak Welsh to.

Susan knows me as one who doesn't often buy presents or flowers for her, but once Carol and Judith, the two nurses, decided to buy her a CD of a favourite singer which they wrapped up into a colourful parcel. When she received it she was shocked, thinking it was from me, that I had been misbehaving and was trying to make it up to her.

As thinks got better I came to know more and more of the staff, and more and more nurses came to see me since I required less specialist attention as time wore on.

ii

I was 18 when I decided that joining the army would be the next move for me. I passed my medical A1, and so all that was left for me to do was to sign on the dotted line and I'd be there. I wonder what would have become of me had I done so. Without a doubt my life, my fate even, would have been quite different to what it is now, but there's no point in thinking about it; I didn't sign up after all and so I didn't go into the army, and that was that. Nain's words and personality were stronger than any army, and my conscience told me that she was right and that it was only fair that I repaid them as best I could for their loving care and the home that they had given me.

Besides I loved farming, and as I also played football and darts and went out with the lads I had the best of both worlds. I'd probably still be farming but for the fact that the owner, Glasebrook, died and the farm was sold.

Gradually, as I grew up and Taid grew older, he gave me more and more responsibility. Glasebrook had another big farm near Denbigh, a farm of 4,000 acres, and it was me, not Taid, who'd go down to Dyffryn Clwyd with the Land Rover and trailer to help in the corn harvesting and to bring a load of straw back with me to Botegir every night. Taking more responsibility meant deciding how much oats was needed, how much sugar beet, making sure that there was enough animal food available and ordering more when it was required. Almost without realising it, I learnt to read and write whilst learning to farm. They were conveyed to me as useless chores in school, but a necessity in farming. I would take calls from William Shaw, the manager, every Monday morning and act on his orders, weighing and selecting lambs for the market in St Asaph at the behest of Len Edwards, the shepherd. During this period I also learnt to work the dogs, essential on a big farm like Botegir.

As I shouldered more and more responsibility, Taid took less and less and would get up later than he had been used to, but Nain would still get up at half past five every morning and cook me a full breakfast before I went out. Bob had been killed on the tractor when I was twelve and for a while after that I had to make do with cutting the thistles with a scythe as Bob's death had affected Taid badly.

I managed to overturn a tractor myself later on, and in the very same field. Unlike Bob's tractor there was a safety frame on this one, but I think that what kept me alive was that I stayed in the seat and held on to the steering-wheel while Bob had tried to jump off and the tractor had rolled over on top of him.

It was during this time that the Nantglyn and District Football League was started by some man from Nantglyn, and I was playing for Bodfari before going on to establish a team in Llanfihangel. There was a good gang of lads there at that time and I still remember most of them: Dei Ty'n Gilfach and Ned Fodwen, two brothers who lived on different farms; Wyn and Robin Gweinidog who were also brothers; Alun Ty'n Celyn; Deio Edwards; Cliff Jiff from Dinmael, and a few others. We'd go to venues such as Llanddulas, Llanfair Talhaiarn, Nantglyn and Llansannan to play. We were allowed to use Cerrig's show field to play home games as we didn't have a suitable pitch in Llanfihangel.

To be honest we were quite a rough gang and I remember one very heated game against Llanddulas when we lost by two goals to one. Their members were all English – at least they spoke English. By now I was the team captain and manager and before they came to Cerrig for a return match I got everyone together and insisted that there wasn't to be any fighting or any misbehaving until the last 15 minutes, and if things got bad that they were all to support one other. It sounded like the preparation for a rugby match – or a war!

During the first five minutes Wyn Gweinidog went up to one of the Llanddulas lads and punched him in the face because of something he'd done, and things got very messy after that. The referee was Oswyn Williams, the Melin y Wig schoolmaster, and he was standing in the middle of the pitch whistling and whistling but no one took any notice of him. He finally walked off the field, threatening never to return. But return he did!

I was in the team for two years, maybe three, and during that period I met a man called Chris Pen Banc, Christopher Price, who was suffering from spina bifida, and would regularly come to watch us play. He had a car for the disabled, a blue three-wheeler and he'd go everywhere in it.

He asked me if I would help him raise money for research into spina bifida by taking part in the pram race on Llandudno promenade. And so we started collecting money and I organized a team, mainly of football lads, who welded two wheelchairs together to make the pram and we competed against nine or ten other teams, including firemen and soldiers.

It was similar to a relay race, the team members would be scattered here and there along the promenade; one would push the pram for a short distance, then another would take over and so on from one end of the promenade to the other. I remember that Caerwyn Carregberfedd was the one in the pram and that Dei Ty'n Gilfach was the first pusher. He was a big, tall lad weighing around 20 stone and he would stop at nothing. Off he went like a bat out of hell, cursing and swearing as he pushed, and the spectators had to scramble out of his way. They yelled at him in English but Dei didn't understand what they were saying! About 20 yards before reaching Ned Fodwen, the next pusher, he let go of the pram and it sped towards the sea and Ned caught it just before it got to the beach. But we won and raised over £3,000 for the cause.

We did this for three years and won every time. In the fourth year we received a letter from the charity kindly asking us not to compete again as other teams were refusing to take part, including the firemen, because they didn't visualise having any hope of winning!

I went to Pen Banc to see Chris almost every Monday night; his father was a forester and his mother was a huge woman weighing about 25 stone because she contracted some disease when Chris was born. Everyone was scared of her, but she was very kind once you got to know her. Chris insisted on learning to drive a real car and his father had an old Austin Cambridge left to rust in the field. He managed to repair it and get it going, and I would go driving with Chris along the narrow lanes and the forest roads in Clocaenog. He was a most dangerous driver because he had lost both his heels to gangrene, and he always drove as if he were in a rally, so we were in the ditch more than we were on the road. Finally I persuaded him to learn to drive an automatic car, which he did, and he passed his test at the first attempt and was a much safer driver after that.

I carried on drinking and driving, passed the breathalyzer test a few times, and thought I was immune. But I eventually had my comeuppance. I had been out with the lads one weekend and was driving into Bodfari when a woman who was taking her dog for a walk stepped off the pavement in front of me, near the 40 miles an hour sign. I had to hit one of the two, the woman or the sign, so I chose the sign and smashed the car into it until the drive shaft was sticking out of its side. It wouldn't move and I had to abandon it. But at least it wasn't on the highway.

After the shock I went to the Downing Arms for a few pints in order to steady my nerves, and by the time I got home that night someone had reported that a car had been in an accident, and the police were waiting for me. Because I had been drinking after the accident I could have escaped without charge but the beer had loosened my tongue, and I foolishly admitted that I had been drinking before driving. So they took me to the police station in Denbigh, and later on in the month I appeared before the magistrates court in Prestatyn where I received a fine of a £100 and was banned from driving for a year. But things could have been worse, the fine bigger and the ban longer. I was quite lucky; I received a yellow not a red card. It was back to the bike and lifts from the lads after that.

I think Taid was quite glad that I had been caught. He knew that I used to drink and drive and he was relieved that nothing worse had happened and that nobody had been hurt. But I didn't learn my lesson, and during the next five years I played football and darts, still drank and had fun with the lads.

During this time Cerrig had an excellent football team and the members were very good to me, picking me up and taking me home because I wasn't allowed to drive. It was Dei Rich who got the team together: Martin Lloyd, Penmachno in goal; Ian Vaughan Evans, Gwyddelwern (who would drive along the back road over Glan Gors to Betws to pick me up in Botegir); Glyn Lloyd from Cyffylliog, the centre half; Dei Rich, sweeper and player manager; Iolo Ystrad Llangwm; Glyn Lloyd from Glasfryn; Dyfrig Howatson from Llangernyw; Roy and Glyn Doctor, Dr Edward Davies's sons, Cerrig; Glyn Traws; and myself as centre forward. We were together every weekend and were always out enjoying ourselves until the early hours of Sunday morning.

Losing my licence had its compensations, because I could train during the summer months by going on my bike, and at the same time I would call at the Lion or Saracens or Queens in Cerrig, then down the A5 to the Goat in Maerdy where I would meet Deio Edwards, my future brother-in-law.

Deio worked in the Creamery in Corwen and on Thursday evenings would go around on his motorcycle selling cheese before meeting me in the Goat Hotel where we played dominoes with the landlady until the early hours of the morning. Then he would take me home, along the narrow road to Betws and then across to Llanfihangel with me on the pillion carrying my bike on my shoulders. No one could risk doing that today!

I'd often go out with him on Saturday nights as well as we were good friends. In fact it was through our friendship that he met Joyce. I had planned to meet him in Llandudno after the pram race and Joyce was with me having driven me to Llandudno. After we won, our team went to the big party, the presentation night that was held at the St George's Hotel, a very posh hotel, where in truth we looked like a gang of hooligans. I told Deio that I had a sister who could drink pint for pint with him. He didn't believe me, but by the end of the night it wasn't

Joyce who was under the table. The lads had come to Llandudno on a bus and Joyce and I had to go home with them that night, leaving the car in Llandudno. She married Deio in 1978, a few months after I'd regained my driving licence.

iii

Yogi's stay in Southport was a very busy period for me. Apart from going regularly back and forth to the hospital I had to press on with planning the changes to the house. At the same time the fund set up by the local rugby club, the Bryan Davies Appeal Fund, was going from strength to strength.

Adapting the house was no simple matter, it entailed much more than making plans and finding a builder. I had to consult with so many agencies and they all had a say in the process – the Health Board, the local Trust, Social Services and the Care Managers at the Southport Hospital. They would not discharge him until they were satisfied with all the arrangements made for him at home.

I made sure that I asked the advice of all the interested parties so that everything would be right from the very beginning and that there would be no unfortunate comebacks along the way. Paul Morgan was appointed to oversee the adapting and building work, to prepare the lift and the hoisting system, and all the other numerous technical gadgets that were needed.

Being a policewoman I was used to visiting all kinds of homes, including the homes of disabled people, and I was determined that our house would be as normal as possible. I would certainly not tolerate a living room filled with disabled persons' aids and equipment with a bed stuck in the corner. Yogi's needs were my priority; I would make sure that an upstairs room would be suitable for him with the rest of the house accessible with wooden floors throughout instead of carpets. Both the children were at a sensitive age and would need as normal an environment as possible to get on with their lives. Then there were the members of staff, those who between them would be spending 24 hours of every day in the house. We had to consider them as well as our own family life, and endeavour to make everyone feel comfortable in a difficult situation.

While concentrating on Yogi, the children and the staff, I forgot to include one person in the equation – myself, and I still have nowhere in the house that I can call my own. And that has been a great disadvantage. But I've managed to let off steam and come to terms with my situation by using the web to chronicle my thoughts and writing a diary which includes thoughts as well as deeds.

I've been surprised by the number of people who have called here. Chief Constable Richard Brunston knocked on the door in mid June 2009 (Pryf Copyn – spider – to give him his bardic name). He learnt Welsh when he came to Wales and was honoured by being made a member of the Bardic Circle of the National Eisteddfod. I was glad to see him and to have the opportunity to thank him personally for the support we'd had from the North Wales Constabulary in the fortnight following the accident. A very kind and friendly man and we, as a family, are indebted to him.

The Southport period was also the fundraising period. It all started when the local rugby club wrote to all Welsh clubs who were members of the Union, and the money came flooding in: small sums, large sums – donations from £20 to large cheques for hundreds, sometimes thousands of pounds. I was amazed at Yogi's reaction to all this. He has never been a very emotional person, but every time I recounted some fundraising event that had taken place there would be tears in his eyes and he couldn't understand why people went to all the trouble to organise events in order to raise money for him.

I would tell him that it was the community's way of thanking him for all that he had done over the years, and how much they appreciated his diligence and devotion to training the children and young people of Bala. He put in hours and hours of his time, on his own, to this work and never complained. By now seven or eight people do what Yogi used to do on his own, and Tony Parry often grumbles when one of them fails to turn up for a training session. But he never expected anything back for his hard work. More than one of the club members have said that if the accident had happened to them, there would have been none of this fundraising, but because Yogi is Yogi…When we are out and about we often come across people who know who Yogi is although they have never seen him.

He is, of course, very conscious of the fact that people who have never met him but have heard of his accident, have a terrible shock when they see him. Often people are scared of coming to see him, but once they have, they can't seem to keep away. I have seen several strong men break down in tears at the sight of him. But there are fewer visitors now that he is home, people have realised that he needs time for himself and his family.

As time passes one forgets what he was like before the accident. I find it difficult sometimes when things aren't going smoothly. It happens to us all, something bothering us, something disturbing the equilibrium, and we shut the door on the problem and walk away. Yogi can't do that. He sometimes insists that life is cruel and that hurts me. This usually happens in the morning when I am leaving the house to go to work, not a good time to have your mind in a turmoil.

Of course this doesn't happen every day, or every week even, but it does happen occasionally, and when people ask how he is I have to say the usual, 'Oh, he's up and down you know,' or 'he's taking it one day at a time,' and that sort of thing. Sometimes after he's had a bad period and I have given the usual response to people's questions, he is suddenly better and those selfsame people see him out and about in town in his wheelchair, and they must then think that I am making a lot of fuss for nothing!

He can change so quickly, and it is often a matter of temperature. We have to keep his temperature constant at about 37 degrees and that is sometimes difficult. And when he says these dreadful things about life being so cruel, it is the pain talking, the pain and the spasms that plague him.

I sleep in his room and some mornings I could happily strangle him. He complains that he has hardly slept because of my snoring! But I don't tell him that I find it hard to sleep because the carers are in and out all night and the machines keep me awake. I don't complain, I don't say anything, it is so much better to have him here at home rather than in a nursing home or hospital.

CHAPTER 5

In the Ruck

i

Nothing stands still in hospital, although time drags and the days seem to go on for ever. I have mentioned regaining my voice and getting rid of the halo and the peg from my stomach. They were all uncomfortable experiences. But one of the worst was getting out of bed and into a chair.

I was flat on my back for weeks. My body's diaphragm did not allow me to sit up, but it was something I had to face up to, indeed this became a necessity since low blood pressure could be a big problem. So the time came when I had to make the effort to sit up, and it sounds so easy, but for me it was a major operation.

Many attempts were made to raise me up before success was achieved, including using a sling which operated like a crane to lift me. The hoist above my bed was a moveable not a permanent one and this made it more difficult. Talk about seeing stars. The first time they succeeded in raising me up and putting me in the chair I went out like a light.

The problem was my blood pressure. It was low because I was lying in bed 24 hours a day. So they tried to improve matters by lifting me up into a sitting position in bed for a short time every day, nevertheless getting me into a chair was a shock to my system and played havoc with my pressure. That's why I passed out.

Finally success was achieved and at first I would spend about 20 minutes in the chair, the periods being gradually increased five minutes at a time so that my body acclimatised to the change and my heart and blood behaved as normally as possible.

I could not for the life of me understand what was happening to my body and this was a most peculiar sensation. It was as if it belonged to someone else. The trouble again was my blood, moving about in my body, flowing from my head to my toes when I was upright, and from my toes to my head when I was lying down, with the pressure varying a great deal from high to low.

The next development, coming about at the beginning of August I think, was to go to the gym, and this was a huge step forward. If lifting me into the chair caused havoc with my blood pressure, getting me to stand up was worse still. But lying in bed all the time had given rise to a great problem, it meant that my heart didn't have to work hard, so more pressure had to be put on it to increase its effectiveness. The way they did this was to stand me in the gym for an hour every day, and at first it was a most unpleasant experience. For the first 15 minutes I could feel the blood flowing into my feet and they felt like lead whilst my heart was beating as if it were intent on leaping out of my chest. But then gradually everything settled and slowed down until it was time for the reversal, as it was called, that is placing me back in bed so that the blood normalised itself. This was also a bad experience causing me dizzy spells and severe headaches.

Standing up was a problem, lying down was a problem, but the greatest problem of all was sitting still in the chair. And it remains a problem. Believe me, it isn't easy to sit still in the same place, unable to move about having been, when I was fit, a restless creature hardly ever sitting down.

It's better not to dwell too much on bodily matters, suffice to say that I had no control over my body after the accident, and so it remains. For weeks on end I was none the wiser that I couldn't accomplish normal bodily functions as I had no idea where I was. But gradually, as I slowly recovered, and my intake of tablets decreased, I became more aware of my situation and realised that I would have to endure a catheter and bag for the rest of my life. It was a most humiliating experience at first, and for a time when I eventually got home.

In hospital, at least, everyone in the ward faced the same

situation, and we accepted things as they were, although it was difficult to adjust to the idea that a different person dealt with you each day. But we were all in the same boat so to speak, and the medical staff were of course well used to these circumstances and could make it easier for us. There was much leg pulling and lewd comments and the staff didn't make you feel different, and so gradually I came to accept my condition. The only problem was our mood, every one different from day to day, and sometimes something said and accepted today would cause offence the next day. This made it difficult for the staff. Perhaps today one of us would accept that we had to have a certain medicine or treatment and refuse the selfsame treatment the next. It was pain that caused such vagaries and made us react as we did. Having said that the greatest pain was in the mind.

Coming home was a different matter. New surroundings, new people around me and, like the rest of the family, having to adapt to circumstances that did not exist before I went into hospital. By now everyone has accepted the situation and I have got used to my carers and they to me.

I had periods of depression in Southport, but I would always try to remember that I promised the doctors when they came to see me in Wrexham that I would strive as best as I could to get better, and that it was on those terms that I was admitted. Friends who came to visit also helped a great deal.

I have mentioned going to the gym, a procedure which took at least two hours and afterwards I would be completely exhausted and would spend the rest of the day flat on my back. I would endeavour to the best of my ability to hide my fatigue from all visitors including Susan and the children. The three usually came on Saturday and I would spend Thursday and Friday resting so that I could appear at my best for their visit. And I would be fine whilst they were with me, but then on the Sunday, completely washed out after such an effort.

Receiving visitors was a blessing, breaking the monotony of the long days, but they were a problem when I was tired or in pain. But I never refused to see anyone. Having made the effort to come all the way from the Bala area, the least I could do was to see them. I have a faint recollection of three friends from Cerrigydrudion coming to see me once – Osian Pentre Draw, Al Bach (Little Al – not the one who had gained the karate belt) and Ioan Bwlch, and I wasn't myself at all. I am still unsure whether they were actually there or whether I had imagined their visit, I was in such pain and dark clouds hung over me, and yet striving as best I could to act as normally as possible whilst they were there.

Every six weeks or so four friends from Llangwm would come to see me – Dewi Disgarth, Llŷr Aeddren, Glennydd Groesfaen and Ilan Tŷ Newydd, setting out from Llangwm after work and arriving at about eight, and if I was in a good mood they'd stay for two or three hours because there were no set visiting hours. This meant their arriving home well after midnight, quite an effort on their part which I fully appreciated. They would sense immediately if I was not myself, and would never overstay their welcome.

During this period of slow but steady progress the staff decided to organise a barbecue once a month, and the first one coincided with a visit by Dilwyn Morgan, John Evans Plas Coch and Rhys Jones Llandrillo. They were overjoyed to see so much food and drink and Rhys had to endure the other two's constant jibes because he was driving and could not have a drink. He however contributed £10 towards the proceedings. John Evans opened a can of Guinness for me and since it had been shaken about it spurted all over the bed clothes making a hell of a mess, and I had to pretend to the staff that someone had spilled the gravy at supper time. I christened them the three wise men, a description that was way-off the truth. After departing Rhys had to return to borrow £3 in order to get out of the car park. All three were skint! But their visit was a tonic, three faithful friends from my early rugby playing days.

A month later the second barbecue was held, and as all the lads had heard about it they came to see me that evening – about

15 of them. The staff had never witnessed anything like it and the food and drink soon disappeared. But the organisers soon learnt their lesson, and in future all those who attended would have to obtain a ticket with 'food for one guest' printed on it. Any number could come to the barbecue but they had to share one platter of food between them!

As I was getting better, children apart from my own would come visiting, and many like the Fron Isa family from Llangwm were very loyal to me; they would come to Southport and make a day of it. During the period of striving to recover as best I could, the visits of friends and families was a great source of strength and comfort, raising my spirits and convincing me that the effort was worth it. I was still in the ruck however, in the thick of things and there was still some time to go before I would be in open territory again.

ii

I lost my driving licence for a year, and those twelve months stand out in my mind because my bike became as important to me then as it had been in the period before I passed my test.

I remember leaving my bike at the Crown in Llanfihangel before going, one Sunday afternoon, to Rhyl with the Summer League lads, my companions during the summer months. We went to the cinema and then did a round of the pubs before returning to the Crown in Llanfihangel in the evening. There we started challenging each other as young lads fuelled with Dutch courage do. I placed my bike on the wall of the bridge high above the Alwen river and was challenged to ride along it from the Crown across to the other side. Falling into the river at that spot could have killed me, but as it happens I kept my balance and managed to ride from one side to the other without mishap, something which I would never have attempted or achieved had I been sober.

During those pre-adult years we were always daring each other to do stupid things, and I've thought a lot lately about how ironic it is that I didn't end up in a wheelchair years ago doing stupid things, but rather as a result of doing something that was quite legitimate and acceptable.

Another memory is of going on a rugby trip to Scotland with Gerallt Llaethwryd and Aeron Maesmor. We travelled in Aeron's car to Wrexham and joined the bus there, stealing a milk churn on the way through Corwen as there would be no toilet on the bus. I knew a few of the lads from Llangollen who were on the same bus and as we were drinking during the journey the milk churn came in very handy!

Somewhere on the M6 the emergency door was opened and the churn's content was emptied while the bus was still moving and the liquid blew in the wind drenching the cars behind us! We were a pretty naughty and irresponsible bunch then.

In Edinburgh the Llangollen lads were staying in a hotel but we were in a bed and breakfast guest house and after a late night out on the town, one of the Llangollen lads, John, became hopelessly drunk. He couldn't stand and I had to half carry him back to the hotel. That's why I was walking back alone to my accommodation quite some distance away, at four in the morning. Suddenly a man came up to me and asked for a light for his cigarette, something that I didn't have as I had never smoked. He started talking, and I soon realised that he was gay. He grabbed my arm and invited me back to his place. I was very useful with my fists at that time and thought that they were the answer to most problems, so I gave him one of my special uppercuts which left him lying flat on his back on the pavement, bleeding and out for the count. I was in shock and thought I had killed him, he was so still. In my panic I ran back to the guest house and blurted out to the others what I had done. The most stupid thing I ever did, because the leg pulling went on unabated throughout the weekend.

Although I'd had a terrible fright because I thought I had killed him, none of us went out to help him. I was persuaded that he would be fine and the following morning as we went past the place on our way to Murrayfield there was no sign of him although his blood was still on the pavement. I got hold of John from Llangollen to let him know how lucky he had been that it wasn't he who was alone that night, or goodness knows what would have happened to him, but he would have been none the wiser as he was in such a state.

The three of us, Gerallt, Aeron and myself returned from Wrexham in Aeron's car and on the way the clutch broke so he had to drive all the way in the same gear. Our only hope of reaching home was to keep on going without stopping, but the traffic lights in Ty'n Cefn could be a problem unless they were on green. They weren't, they were on red, and I had to jump out to stop the traffic so that our car could get through, then I ran after it up the A5!

My companions during the winter months were Cerrig lads, and over the years the Cerrig football team developed into a good one, reaching the peak of its success during the two seasons: 1979–80 and 1980–81. During 1979–80 I won three trophies with the club: one for being the club's main scorer, one when the team came second in the league, and one for winning the Challenge Cup. The following year we won the League and the Cup – the Jack Owen Cup.

Following that win the team was invited to Llandudno for the presentation ceremony. So on a Friday evening at the end of the season, 30 of us went in a hired coach from Cerrig to the British Legion's Club in Llandudno and there we had a night to remember, a night that ended for three of us at around seven thirty on Saturday morning.

After the presentation we asked the doorman what time they were closing and when he said half past ten, hours too early for us to be even thinking about going home, we decided to go to the Winter Gardens, a nightclub in town, which would remain open way beyond ten thirty. We walked down in twos and threes and some of the lads started dancing with the girls there. I went to the bar to get a drink and I was standing there when a huge crowd of Scousers turned up, about 60 of them, and soon after that things got quite wild!

The Scousers objected to our lads dancing with the girls, and that's probably what caused the trouble. Be that as it may, one or two fights broke out on the dance floor and I was standing at the bar laughing when somebody suddenly punched me in the face, a blow which resulted in a huge black eye.

Things soon got out of hand – chairs and tables were hurled around, girls threw glasses on the floor so there were pieces of glass everywhere and those who fell got nasty cuts. It was a proper free-for-all, and the principle was, if you didn't recognise someone, then he must be one of the enemy and there to be clobbered.

The only bouncer present tried to gain control of the situation. He grabbed a chair leg and hit Al Bach, one of our smallest lads, with it. Unfortunately, the bouncer didn't realise that he had made the wrong choice and that Al Bach had a black belt in karate, and the next thing I saw was the chair leg going in one direction and the bouncer in the other.

Eventually the police arrived, after a long scene reminiscent of a saloon fight in a cowboy film. Slowly but surely it all came to an end, a number of the Scousers having to go to hospital as well as one of our lads, Emyr Wyn, Traian. He had fallen and a piece of glass had pierced his knee. The police got hold of our bus and ordered the driver to bring it to the club door, and then we were herded like sheep into it by a huge six-foot tall sergeant, without his helmet, acting like a sheep dog, or a shepherd!

After getting us all on the bus he said: 'That's the best thing that's happened in this place. Those Scousers have been coming here for three weekends on the trot, and have caused trouble every time. Thank you very much,' he said. 'We'll get no more trouble from them. Now go home and don't ever bloody come back again.'

So we were allowed to go home without anyone being punished, but the night wasn't over for three of us. It's was between two and three in the morning when we arrived in Cerrig where Med Fodwen had left his car, a blue Triumph Stag in the square, and that's how Dei Ty'n Gilfach and I got home to Llanfihangel. As we were travelling towards the village in the dead of night, we saw a light in the sky over the Clocaenog Forest. We decided to go and check it out, thinking at the same time that we could be imagining things.

It was lucky that we were nosy parkers and that we doubted ourselves that night, because the forest was on fire, and the fire was moving rapidly down towards Tan y Graig farm where a large family lived. We raced back to Llanfihangel to call the fire brigade and said that we would wait for them on the bridge to show them where to go as we knew the forest roads like the back of our hands. The three of us were sitting on the wall by the Crown in the village when the first one arrived, from Cerrig, and then another two – one from Corwen and the last from Ruthin. We helped them douse the fire and it was eventually brought under control before it reached the farm buildings at Tan y Graig.

It was close to half past eight in the morning when Med drove me into the yard at Botegir, and because Taid was standing outside he dropped me off quickly, did a handbrake turn and rallied away noisily. I had fallen in the forest and burned my trousers and shoes and ripped my shirt, I had been in thick smoke, and I had a black eye as well. I must have looked a hell of a sight. When I walked into the house Nain immediately came to the conclusion that I had been drinking and had been in trouble, although it was difficult for her to believe that about me because to her I was usually an angel. But that morning she gave me a real telling off and refused to believe the story about the fire. There was nothing I could do but turn my back on her, change, and go to work without breakfast.

The following Saturday, Taid and Nain both went to Cerrig as usual – Taid to the Queens to play dominos with his friends, and Nain to the shops. They heard the story about the fighting in Llandudno, but nothing about the fire in Clocaenog. That Saturday night I went out as usual and an interesting fact was that the lads who were married were nowhere to be seen, they were confined to barracks by their wives for some weeks after that!

Within a month I received a letter of thanks from a North Wales officer of the fire brigade and a cheque for £20 towards the cost of buying new clothes, a very generous remuneration at that time. All three of us received the same letter. Nain didn't know what to say after she had wrongly given me a bollocking for being drunk that night. As I said, she thought I was an angel; we had that special relationship that often exists between a grandmother and her grandson. She would often threaten, but her bark was worse than her bite. But I was back in her good books after playing my part in preventing the fire in the forest from spreading.

Sometime during the beginning of the 1980s Cerrig's excellent team was on the decline. The Ruthin club persuaded Dei Rich to become their manager and, as every other manager does, he took many of the players with him, including Roy Doctor, Iolo Ystrad and myself, and I played for the town for two or three seasons.

In 1983, Nain died. As far as I knew she had never been to see the doctor in her life; she had definitely not been in hospital. But she had started complaining that she was tired all the time and I never took much notice of that, thinking that it was her age catching up with her. She still got up at half past five in the morning, but eventually I managed to convince her that she should go to see the doctor, and he sent her to Wrexham for some tests. Persuading her to go to Wrexham was a major operation for Taid and me, but we finally succeeded and she was found to be suffering from leukaemia. There was no cure for it then, only new drugs that could slow down the condition. We converted the old parlour into a bedroom for her so that she wouldn't have to climb the stairs, but she quickly deteriorated, and died in December of that year. Her death affected me badly. We had been such good mates, and her death was a severe blow. I went off the rails completely for a while.

Taid, Haydn the youngest brother, and I still lived on the farm, but there was nobody to cook or wash our clothes or cater for any of our needs. We had to fend for ourselves. Taid had been completely spoilt over the years and he had never washed a cup in his life, so he had no idea what to do. Now it was I who had to get up to make the breakfast, and he would get up at eight. I made porridge every morning and put it in the Aga to keep it hot until he got up. I took over the task of looking after him, cooking, washing, ironing and cleaning.

The kitchen floor was of traditional blue slabs. Taid had been smoking a pipe since he was nine years old, smoking Condor and St Bruno. He had lost the third finger on his right hand when riding a motorbike in his youth, when somebody opened a car door as he was passing and knocked him over. He therefore had trouble shredding the tobacco in his hand and loading it into his pipe, dropping most of it on the floor. He would also, after lighting his pipe, throw the match towards the fire and it would often land on the floor. It was lucky that we didn't have a carpet.

I found it sad that none of his children came to look after him, or even visit him very often either. Taid and Nain had five children – well, four to be precise: Trefor, who lived in Australia and who died young; Jini, the eldest daughter, who lived in Rochdale; Mam, who lived in Bodfari; Medwyn who lived in Betws and Haydn, the youngest, who lived with us in Botegir. It was when we had buried Nain and I was going through her papers that I learnt that Haydn was in fact Jini's son born out of wedlock, and brought up as one of Taid and Nain's children.

What made me very angry was that everyone came to Botegir when Nain died, snivelling and crying, and yet no one had taken much interest when she was alive. Mam would come to Botegir occasionally after Nain's death, when I'd go to fetch her, but that didn't last long.

And so the three of us settled down, Taid and me, and Haydn whom I now knew to be my cousin. No thought of marriage entered my mind, although I had been seeing a girl from Pentrefoelas on and off for about ten years, and to be honest, I treated her like dirt – almost the only thing that I am genuinely ashamed of in my life. Guys my age were married, many of them in their twenties, and she wanted to come to live with me in Botegir. I would say that it wasn't fair expecting her to look after the three of us and we often disagreed about that. We would fall out from time to time and then get back together, but I knew that it wouldn't work for us.

After losing Nain, I hit the bottle harder than ever, and looked for any excuse to be away from home. I went with Aelwyd Llangwm quite often to eisteddfodau and concerts, not because I was interested but only for the trips and for the opportunities to chase the girls. I was really out of control for quite a time.

iii

During Yogi's stay in Southport I kept a diary on our website. It was often a relief just before bedtime to record the events of the day and sometimes lash out at all and sundry to get rid of my frustrations. I didn't write every day but on some days I would visit the website more than once.

And it was good to get other people's reactions to my thoughts; it was also a good way of keeping in touch with my friends as several of them would respond and leave their own messages. Unfortunately, I soon began to receive indecent messages, scores of them and I got very upset, until Buddug from Boyns – the computer company – managed to block them all.

What I have written helps me to remember all the little details that one forgets and reminds me of how I felt at any particular time. I sometimes felt utterly lost, having to do everything on my own, simple family chores like taking the children to football, swimming lessons and piano lessons. Yogi always used to do these things and, in the first weeks following the accident, I soon came to realise that you can't take anything for granted, you have to appreciate everything you have because you never know what lies around the corner.

The days and months after the move to Southport were filled with the usual family routine and visits to the hospital. We managed to get him a television set which worked well, and we tried to make his corner of the ward more like home by placing pictures of Ilan and Teleri by the bed where he could see them, and sticking cards they had made on the wall. And then, hanging proudly above his head, the Welsh Dragon which Dilwyn Morgan (Porc) had sent him.

I used to feed him when I was there, and there was nothing wrong with his appetite. It was easy to feed him with a fork or spoon, but if he was having sandwiches it became quite dangerous – his teeth were as sharp as a dog's! I then had to face the long trek home and the children waiting for their supper. This was a daunting and anxious time and throughout it all I had to struggle to keep my own and everyone else's spirits up. Then suddenly some small event would lighten up the day, such as the day towards the end of June, when, after weeks of trying to read the signs, reading his lips and interpreting the movements of his head and eyes, he suddenly spoke for five whole minutes. An enormous effort on his part but worth every second.

When I returned the following day, Yogi was all smiles, his voice was back and sounding pretty normal except that he sounded as if he had a sore throat. And the good news was that he had his own voice and would not need a voice box. And that was when the trick was played on Tony Parry (TP).

The website was very useful when I wanted to send messages to his friends and this is what I wrote sometime in July:

> As Yogi is so far from home I think he could do with more visitors. You will appreciate that while he is still in the Intensive Care Unit he only needs to see the people he has done a lot with in recent months plus family and close friends. Tony (Parry) has a visitors' rota, and it would be a shame if it started to shrink.

Yogi naturally had his ups and downs, and when the black clouds threatened he could visualise no future for himself. That's when visits from his friends were a great help. For one thing he had to make the effort to be cheerful in their presence, and on the other hand they themselves were a tonic because of their wit and humour.

I myself grabbed every chance to break the monotony of his days by involving the children as often as possible. One example was Father's Day on 2 June 2007 when they had the opportunity to thank their father for all he had done for them. His leadership and advice has been priceless, and thankfully he is still with us to advise and lead the way if not to undertake the usual family chores.

On that particular Sunday Ilan and Teleri read out their cards to him and presented him with a cup – No. 1 Dad – a cup which meant more to him than any he had won playing football and rugby. Then we had a celebration lunch – Welsh lamb, new potatoes and cabbage, with Yogi insisting that the coleslaw which Ilan had made in school should be mixed into the gravy. He'd given him ten out of ten for it, which was more than he'd had from his teacher!

Yogi was naturally overjoyed to see the children and they loved to visit him, and sometimes very funny things happened like the time Teleri asked her father to sponsor her on an arranged walk to raise money for his fund!

All these things sound so normal and simple, but normality is so important in everyday life, simple things that are vital to sustain us and keep the family unit as close as it has always been. It is the normal things that get lost in life when a situation causes everything to be anything but. And it was so important for us all to look to the future. Even when he was still in Intensive Care, Yogi had already said he fully intended to return to Maes Gwyniad to train the junior team once he was home. It was no wonder that the doctors at Southport were happy with his development and the way he faced his situation.

He would usually see the lighter side of things and enjoyed laughing and leg pulling. He once told me that when he was asleep one afternoon he had woken up to see someone with a tape measure measuring him for a wheelchair. I told him that the time for him to begin worrying was when he woke up to find Dei and Eryl Evans (the Bala undertakers) measuring him!

Another time, when Yogi had been taken to the gym and

placed on a bed that was raised so that he looked as if he was standing, for an hour at a time, I told him I'd had an idea to suggest to the police. Yogi looked puzzled: 'We could tour the country as a double act,' I said. 'You can be trussed up like that and I will throw knives at you and if I happen to hit you it won't matter, because you won't feel the pain'! 'No,' he replied, 'but I will bleed.'

We all feel low sometimes, but the next time it happens to you, why not lie flat on your back in bed and imagine that you can't feel a thing below your neck. That is how life is for Yogi and he seldom complains. Even when he doesn't feel well he still makes an effort. He had a terrible headache one day and when I went to visit him he was lying there with his eyes closed. I went to him and whispered in his ear: 'Is anyone home?' The answer was, 'No, I'm in Aberystwyth.'

Little things became important like the breeze blowing in his face when he came to the door with us for the first time in his wheelchair. The Southport breeze caressing his cheeks meant more to him than the whole world at that moment.

During the summer of 2007 the efforts to raise money for the fund snowballed, and one of the most popular events was the sponsored walk around Lake Alwen. This took place on the last Saturday in June, just when Yogi got his voice back, a very special time for all of us.

The walk was organised by the junior rugby team and they raised £4,000 to £5,000 for the fund. This is how Teleri (Lloyd Roberts) recorded the event:

> We had a really good day. The weather was fine with everybody in good spirits. There were 164 participants all wearing suitable boots with Euros Puw in his wellingtons... Thank you Gwyn Awen Meirion, Geraint and Yvonne for keeping an eye on us all... It was good to witness such a turnout, proof of how much Yogi means to so many of us. Thank you to all the organisers, especially Bethan.

The following day I went to Southport and Yogi was in a good mood. I told him all about the walk and that about 20 had turned up and he was very pleased and wished to thank them all! Then I told him the truth. He was amazed and his eyes filled with tears when he realised that over 160 people had turned out for the event. Then I asked him what he had been doing – a silly question I know – and he said he'd run round the block a few times! No, thankfully, he hadn't lost his sense of humour.

The visiting routine had by now been established. I visited him two or three times during the week and the children came with me at weekends. After a few weeks of going back and forth to Southport like this, I got used to the road, but I was never happy driving on the motorway. Reaching home I would be dead tired but it was always good to have the children's company when they were with me. In the car, on my own, I had time to reflect on all that was happening and what the future held for us.

CHAPTER 6

Ball Change

i

MID SUMMER 2007, four months since my accident and I was slowly improving step by step. The next significant move was to be measured for a chair – 'The chair'! Not a temporary one but a permanent one for use when I got home, an electric chair purpose-built for me and no one else. The usual waiting period for such a chair is two years and, true to form, I had been home for six months before I received it in June 2009.

Being measured for the chair was part of the preparation for my going home, and such an experience raised my spirits and stirred my imagination and I could see myself arriving back in Bala and going to the town in my chair, although it was supposed to be for use in the house only. Then suddenly, something would happen to stall my gradual progress again.

Less than a week after being measured for the chair, Susan and the children visited me, and I had great trouble with my breathing. I felt as if someone was pressing a cushion against my face trying to choke me, but none of the staff would believe me. The machine, they said, was showing that I was receiving the correct amount of air, but I wasn't.

Susan had to send the children away from the unit and call one of the nurses. And not before time, because the pipe was blocked but the machine failed to register it. I dread to think what would have happened had Susan not been there at the time. I felt angry and afraid.

My 50th birthday arrived whilst I was still in Intensive Care, and I never imagined that anything would happen on that day other than visits from Susan and the children who had arranged to stay for a few nights in a flat in the hospital, so that they could be near me. My sister Joyce and her husband Dei called, but only to take the children to the swimming pool in Splashwood, so that I would be left in peace, or that was their excuse. But it wasn't that at all.

Without my knowledge a party had been arranged for me in the day room, and all the food had come from Bala, a real spread prepared by Eleri Wenallt and Linda Penlan and a birthday cake made especially by Rhiannon Ty'n Coed, Rhosygwaliau. I knew nothing about it and yet I had sensed that something was afoot because the nurse on duty that morning had insisted on my shaving and wearing clean clothes, something I wasn't at all keen on!

It was a bank holiday weekend and the traffic was heavy, but they came to the party in great numbers, over 60 of them, travelling in a convoy from Bala; family members, friends, rugby colleagues, every generation represented including a fair number of children.

Apart from Ilan and Teleri the other children had never seen me in a wheelchair, and some of them were startled at first, but they soon got over the initial shock and accepted me as I was.

We had a day to remember, thanks to all those who made it special for me. And the festivities weren't over either because the next day members of Llangwm Male Voice choir arrived, over 40 of them on their way home from Scotland, having made a detour in order to visit me. The effect of the national drink of Scotland on the breath of some of them was almost enough to make me drunk! They sang three or four songs in the ward and it was a wonderful experience to see patients and staff from other wards crowding around my bed to listen to them. They had never seen or heard anything like it before and the choir promised to come back to sing carols before Christmas.

A few days later I had a visit from Dilwyn Morgan, who had interrupted his sponsored bicycle ride from Land's End to John O'Groats in order to see me. I was very pleased to welcome him, but Susan can say more about that, being in touch with him throughout his long ride.

The period following my birthday was a quiet time although between ten and 15 people came to visit me every week, some who came regularly and some only occasionally. One day I had a visit from Sulwen Davies – the mother of Rhian Dafydd who is one of my very loyal friends – and she brought me some bara brith. It raised my spirits to see her, seeing people of an older generation and people who had no connection with the rugby club, people who were not acquainted with me coming to visit. It amazed me to experience so much kindness, concern and goodwill towards me and that in a hospital unit where many of the occupants received hardly any visitors at all. It was very sad for them, and I felt gratified to have such friends and such a family

ii

I went somewhat off the rails after Nain's death, but soon came to my senses. Martin Rhosfaith worked on the door at the Bridge Hotel, Bontuchel on Wednesday and Friday nights when disco parties were held there. He was a bouncer really, and when he asked me if I'd like similar part-time work, I immediately agreed.

About the same time, Mick Ruggiero opened a club in Rhyl – Maxine's – and both of us worked there on Saturday nights. It was shirtsleeve order on Wednesdays and Fridays at the Bridge, but we had the whole penguin look in Rhyl – white shirt and a bow tie.

I really enjoyed my work at both venues, because so many of the customers knew me. Martin and I would drive from Cerrig to Rhyl on Saturday nights, just the two of us, but we returned with a full car load – those who had missed the last bus, or were too drunk to drive.

I drank very little whilst working as a bouncer, and I soon realised that most of those who came to the pub and the club were younger than me. What really brought me to my senses during this period was seeing these youngsters getting so hopelessly drunk and in such a state that they couldn't control themselves.

It suddenly dawned on me that I was much older than most of them and that most of my peers were by now married with children, and here was I acting like a young lad.

The pub in Bontuchel closed fairly early even on disco nights, but not the club in Rhyl! Three or four in the morning was par for the course and, occasionally, following an exceptionally good night, it would be morning. I would then eat breakfast at the club before driving home to work on the farm.

During this time, I signed on to play football for Ruthin, and Bill Grinder, the club chairman, an Irishman and a very friendly bloke, decided to organize a trip to Ireland to play two or three games there.

About 25 of us set out on a Friday night, crossed over on the ferry from Holyhead, and then went by bus to a splendid hotel out somewhere in the country, a hotel that was willing to welcome 25 footballers and their supporters. Among the camp followers was Gerallt Llaethwryd and Ifor Glasfryn, two who didn't play football at all, but one of them had to before the end of the tour!

Another person on the trip was Bryn Jones from Ruthin and, as you can imagine, there was much drinking and jollity on the boat. Bryn was hell-bent on drinking me under the table, so I invited him to join a group of us who were sharing a round, but that didn't please him. He wanted a session only for the two of us, but I declined.

There was a wedding party at the hotel, 300 to 400 guests in a massive room on the ground floor, but our crowd were quite happy in a small bar upstairs.

A group of us started singing, as we always did on such occasions, and when he heard us, the father of the bride came up and invited us to join them to sing to the guests. It was a wonderful party, and by two o'clock in the morning, Bryn was asleep on a sofa, while I was still awake. Drink me under the table indeed!

We were well looked after by John, the hotelier, his wife and their three daughters who ran the hotel as a family business.

The eldest, Pauline, was married, the second engaged, and the youngest served in the bar.

By five o'clock in the morning, I was the only one left in the bar, going on and on about the IRA and Meibion Glyndŵr, and every other topic under the sun because I was so drunk. The youngest daughter was a very shy girl, and seemed very lonely, and she told me that she never went out socialising with anyone. At six o'clock in the morning the mother came down and began to cook breakfast, and I went to help, frying bacon and eggs with one hand, and holding a pint of Guinness in the other. I became very friendly with the family at the time.

The following day we played football and I don't remember much about the game, but I do recall that it was during that weekend that Barry McGuigan, the Irish boxer, won the world championship, and naturally there were celebrations in Ireland. Usually the pubs and hotels would close at twelve on Saturday nights since it was Sunday the following day, but because of the celebrations, there was no closing that Saturday night. So, as happened the previous night, I was still in the bar at five o'clock in the morning, myself and the young barmaid. She told me that she'd had some bad experiences with a boy some years before, and that was the reason that she never went out. I then told her my story – I was 26 years old and she was a mere 16!

The schedule was the same on the Sunday: playing a game during the day and staying awake all night. On Sunday there was a very noisy crowd of up to 400 in a disco downstairs. Monday came and we had another game to play and I had to be in goal. I would be no good anywhere else, and not much use in goal either! So many of the team were ill from drinking too much that Ifor Glasfryn had to play one game, and he did so in his cowboy boots. He had absolutely no idea how to play football!

The hotel family bought a set of four expensive crystal glasses to present to Ruthin Football Club, but they took one of the glasses out of the box and gave it to me, so the club got three and I got the fourth because we had become such good friends.

The reason I tell this story is that six months later, I received a

With my sister Joyce in the early 1960s.

My first love!

On the yard of Botegir Farm, Llanfihangel Glyn Myfyr, in my early teens.

A night out at the Crown in Llanfihangel to celebrate winning the Pram Race for the third time in succession. (In the middle with the Cup)

Pushing the pram in Llandudno Pram Race.

Bodfari's Summer League team, 1979. In the middle, yellow jersey and cap (or was it a bucket?) on my head.

Grandfather Botegir, Harry Roberts.

With my parents, my grandfather (on my father's side) Dei Wils and my great-grandfather and grandmother (on my father's side).

Grandmother Botegir.
I thought the world of her.

Botegir Farm and Grandmother Botegir seen standing in the doorway.

Our wedding day,
25 August, 1990.
I aged a year overnight!

On our honeymoon in Tunisia,
August 1990.

Me, Susan and Ilan, 11 June 1995.

Susan and me at a wedding.

Llanuwchllyn team, winners of the Brewers' Cup, 1995. I'm in the back row, fourth from the right.

Bala rugby team. I'm third on the right, back row.

I'm in the back row, fourth from the left, mid 1990s.

Ifor Williams's football team which competed in the Cynwyd Cup, 2004.

Bala lads.

With Bala's junior team, 2005/06. Tels (Teleri) is third from the left, back row.

With Ilan, summer 1995.

Euro Disney, 2002.

Me, Ilan and Teleri at Caernarfon
airfield, summer 1997.

In Menorca, 1999. Pity the cow!

With Ilan and Teleri, around 2003.

A holiday in the Caribbean, April 2007 – a week before the accident. With my new friend.

With Susan.
Photo: *Daily Post*

Tŷ Ni family with Dic and Morfudd (Susan's parents).

Outside Plas Coch on the day I returned home, 5 November 2008.
Photo: *Daily Post*

The four of us in Southport, 2008.

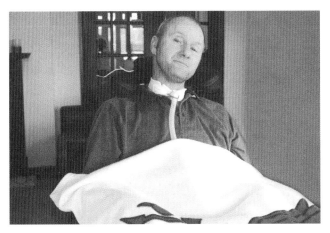

After arriving home,
November 2008.
Photo: *Daily Post*

Photo: *Daily Post*

Tŷ Ni family,
Christmas
2008.
Photo: Erfyl Lloyd
Davies

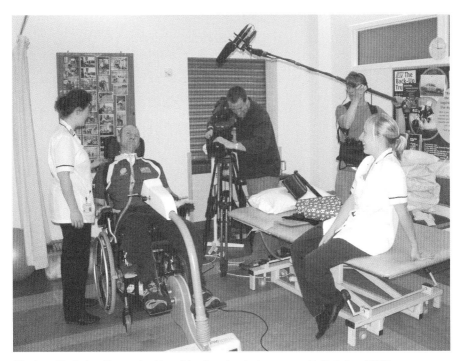

Filming *O'r Galon* (From the Heart) in the physiotherapy unit, October 2007.
Photo: Catrin M S Davies

A bacon butty after returning home.
Photo: *Daily Post*

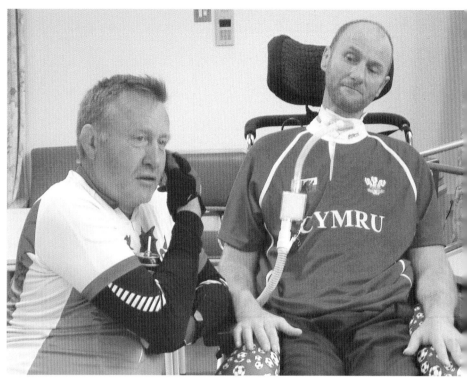

Dilwyn visiting Southport
during his journey from
Land's End to John o' Groats.
Photo: Catrin M S Davies

Dilwyn commencing his
sponsored bike ride.

Home at last!
Photo: *Daily Post*

The Tŷ Ni family with the Olympic torch.

Ilan with the Olympic torch.

Tels doing charity work in Malawi.

Tels doing a sponsored skydive.

letter from the parents thanking me for talking to their youngest daughter, and listening to her story. They had naturally been worried about her, but following our visit she had once again begun to live a normal life, going out with her friends after a long period of staying in and shying away from any socialising. Four years later I received an invitation to her wedding. Naturally I declined, but I wrote a letter thanking them for the invitation and a postscript to her future husband warning him not to ill-treat her or I'd send Meibion Glyndŵr after him! I haven't heard from them in Ireland in years, but I hope she's happy wherever she is.

Ruthin played in a league above Cerrig, the Wrexham Area Division 1. The Cerrig team split up soon afterwards when the Conwy and District League came to an end and a new league –the Subaru League – was formed. Cerrig's problem was that no one would undertake the management of the team following Dei Rich's departure to Ruthin.

I played for two seasons with Ruthin, and was booked or sent off on several occasions. Dei Rich was quite strict as a manager and would insist on our training every week. 'No training, no game' was his command. Once, whilst I was serving a ban he let one lad – I don't remember his name – play, even though he hadn't trained. There's no denying that he was a good player, but I believe it should be one rule for all and I said as much. We didn't argue, and we remain good friends to this day, but because of being constantly booked or banned and also this feeling of unfairness, I decided to leave the club, and came over to Bala to see if I could play for them, as I knew Tubby Edwards, Llanuwchllyn, the manager and several others at the club.

But, of course, I was banned from playing at the time, and a ban carries over from one league to the next, so I couldn't play for anyone until the ban was over.

It being a Saturday night I went to Plas Coch and met Robin Penlan, one of the lads who founded Bala Rugby Football Club. We began talking about football and the fact that I was banned. We chatted about rugby as well, and I was invited to train with the club on the following Tuesday night. I'm a firm believer in training, and I missed it because of the ban.

So on the Tuesday night, off I went to Maes y Gwyniad without an inkling of what to expect as I knew nothing about rugby, I barely knew that the ball wasn't round. The club was a very primitive place – a small generator lit up four weak lamps, and the training ground was no more than thirty square yards in size. Dewi Twm was the trainer; and I didn't realise that his name was Dewi Davies until Ilan went to Ysgol y Berwyn, where he's the headmaster! I remember that Irwyn, Rhys Llandrillo's brother was there, and so was Gwyndaf Hughes and many others.

Someone kicked the ball high in the air and called on me to catch it. I did so, and the next thing there was a bang – three of the Gwern Biseg brothers had tackled me until I was flat on the ground and was covered in mud. I got up to my feet, and the same thing happened again. I caught the ball and got tackled. Looking back I'm convinced that Robin Penlan had arranged it all beforehand.

But I have a very stubborn nature, and I didn't give up, I just kept going. They weren't going to get the better of me. I had no idea who was who but I stood my ground until the end of the training session. There were no changing rooms or washing facilities, so many went home as they were, their rugby kit and boots covered in mud, the others wore their own clothes over their training outfits and headed for Plas Coch, and that's what I did.

So it was a baptism of mud rather than of fire that I had for rugby and, having arrived at Plas Coch, some of them went into a huddle to select the team for the forthcoming Saturday away game in Harlech. They must have been desperate for players during that time because I was selected to play for the first team, in the centre of all positions. I had no knowledge whatsoever of the rules of the game, but thankfully Arwyn Hughes, the other centre, knew them all.

It was resolution rather than knowledge that carried me

through that match. As one of the Harlech players ran past me with the ball and was about to score a try, I tripped him up. I had never heard of the rule that restricted a tackler to using his hands and arms only in a tackle. I'd have tripped him up on the football field, and chanced a reprimand, but things were obviously different here. It all went a bit wild with the Harlech lads furious and some of them fighting with members of the Bala team near the touchline. The referee came up to me and I realised that he was going to send me off, and that during my first match! I apologised profusely and explained that I didn't know that tripping was not allowed. Rhys and Robin knew the referee well and they explained to him that I was playing for the first time and was not familiar with the rules.

Anyway, I was pardoned and allowed to stay on the field, and we beat Harlech. In the clubhouse later on, I bought a pint for the bloke I'd tripped up, and apologised to him, and he was fine about it. That's one of the features of rugby; all hostilities on the playing field are immediately forgotten off the field, and all are united in friendship. We had a very enjoyable evening before returning to Bala, four of us in one car, heading for the Plas Coch until closing time, which was eleven o'clock in those days. Then it was home James for me, having played my first game of rugby – a game that would mean so much to me in future, and one that would completely change my life.

iii

My own aspirations and imaginings about how things would be in the future were very different to stark reality.

Towards the end of June officials from Southport Hospital and from the Local Health Authority came to Tŷ Ni to hear my plans for adapting the house to Yogi's needs. They all thought that what I had in mind was possible but I was soon to realise that there were many things that I had not considered. Yogi would need the services of two intensive carers 24 hours a day and one would have to be up all night. I knew that Yogi would need a lift, but not that the lift would have to be big enough to accommodate the wheelchair and one of the carers. We would need a small generator in case the electricity supply was interrupted, also doors would need widening, ramps built, a special bathroom would have to be fitted out, lifting hoists provided, the list went on and on.

The planning process is a long-drawn-out affair, enough to test the patience of Job, but I thought that a request to adapt a property, especially for a disabled person, even within the National Park would be given preferential treatment and that the work could be started fairly soon.

But it was not to be. In mid August I received a letter from the National Park Authority that made me see red. The letter stated that before any progress could be made I had to have confirmation from Gwynedd's Social Services Department that Yogi was registered as disabled with them.

Yogi of course was in Southport, and hadn't been assessed by Gwynedd's Social Services Department, and there was no chance of that happening for many months. I dreaded to think that he could be ready to come home before anything had been done to the house, which was when we learnt that a lack of applying discretion of any sort was a very common phenomenon in official circles. Yogi lay flat on his back in hospital, paralysed from the neck down, with no hope of recovery, and breathing through a ventilator and yet he had to be assessed for disability!

As a family we have always tried to do everything honestly and by the book, but this sort of response makes me wonder if it pays to be honest. But then again, I can sleep at night.

I decided to ask Margaret (Yogi's case manager) if there was a way around this: a letter from the hospital perhaps. The last thing I needed was to be stuck on the phone for hours being shunted from one person to another trying to solve the problem. But if that was the only way, then it had to be done. I thought of phoning the National Park Authority to ask how much the application would cost and offer to pay for it myself, but then I thought – why should I?

At long last, after innumerable phone calls to explain my

predicament, I was given to understand that I could satisfy the requirements of Section 2 of the National Support Law 1948 (National Aid Statute) by getting a medical consultant in Southport to testify to the seriousness of Yogi's disability. The crisis was over and my blood pressure was back to normal.

It wasn't only at home that I had to fight for Yogi's rights, it had to be done in hospital as well. Fight is perhaps the wrong word to use; it gives a false impression of a hospital and staff that were in reality very supportive and positive in their attitude. But if you don't ask you don't get and towards the end of July 2007, seeing Yogi progressing so well, I reminded the physio that I had mentioned several times that he might benefit from going to the swimming pool. He reacted with astonishment – no one installed with a trachy had ever been near the pool. The various departments must have discussed the matter because the physio came back with the reply that it might be possible towards the end of August after the pool had been repaired.

Yogi, incapacitated as he was, was still most supportive of me. I had been studying for an external degree in Professional Development (Education) at Swansea University and was to receive cap and gown at a ceremony in the city. At best it was difficult to leave Yogi and go home, although I knew he was in safe hands, and I often cried when I was on my own after the children had gone to bed. But to think of going to Swansea – so far away – was a different kettle of fish. But Yogi was determined that I should go. He had encouraged me throughout the time while I was studying. I once lost 2,000 words on the computer and when I told him what had happened, all he said was: 'go back and start again!' Which was exactly what I needed to do. Naturally he insisted on my going to the graduation ceremony.

And so I went to Swansea. Dad and Mam and Teleri came with me (Ilan was in Italy on a school trip). We stayed at the Marriott Hotel and went into town to eat. The ceremony at the Brangwyn Hall was wonderful, a fitting end to a long period of studying and essay writing. Yogi had tears in his eyes when I showed him my picture in cap and gown, and I thanked him for all the support he had given me.

On his birthday, 27 August, we organised a party for him, and the children and I were allowed to stay in a flat at the hospital for two nights, and we were advised to bring him a cap which he could wear if the weather changed. Since the accident Yogi wasn't aware of temperature changes and we constantly had to take his temperature. We still do.

Anyway, I found an old green and black Goofy hat with huge ears and took that with me. The nurses were in hysterics, he looked so funny! But I had a Bala Rugby Club hat tucked in my bag. Anything like that helped to lighten the mood and keep everyone cheerful.

At the end of that week there was a case conference with the Gwynedd Health Authority, Yogi's medical team and its manager, Margaret, to discuss his care once he was home. Everything went well and it was gratifying to know that the Health Authority would do everything in their power to provide the best care possible for him in Tŷ Ni.

Part of the process was to teach me to clean the tube in Yogi's throat, change the trachy and use the 'ambi bag'. I confess that I could never become a nurse, but I try my best and I'll do anything as long as it gets him home.

All this time the spasms seemed to be getting worse. The medical team told me that they would try to control them with tablets and that I should tell his visitors not to touch him during a spasm and not to worry – that they wouldn't last long.

The children went back to school after the summer holidays and during the first week of term a fellow pupil attacked Ilan in the school grounds at lunchtime. Luckily he wasn't badly hurt but it knocked us for six and spread a dark cloud over the whole day. Naturally Yogi was very agitated when he heard of the incident. Some may think it odd that I had told him about it, but we always told each other everything, that's how it has always been with us. Someone visiting him would probably have mentioned the incident anyway and it was better that he heard about it from us.

It was an unfortunate thing to happen, but as a family we were all aware that most of the local young people had supported us wholeheartedly during the last months and it was a shame that one or two individuals had not followed their example. But the day was not without its lighter moments; Nia phoned to say that Dilwyn had arrived at John O'Groats, having successfully cycled all the way from Land's End. But more of that later.

All through July and August and up to Christmas things were developing at home and in the hospital. Yogi was measured for a permanent chair that would be suitable for him at home; he was given a mobile breathing machine which meant that he could move away from his bed; a scan showed that there was no change in the condition of his back. At home the efforts to raise money were gathering pace with events such as Lois' parachute jump, the rugby gala – my first visit to the rugby ground since the accident, and the auction at which I and the children sat at the top table with the President of the Welsh Rugby Union, Glanmor Griffiths. He had himself visited Yogi a few weeks previously with a personal message from John Howard, the Prime Minister of Australia.

The rugby gala and promises auction were good examples of the events organised to raise money for the fund. Over 500 people attended the gala. Two matches were played, one between Bala and Harlech's U-21 teams, and the other between Bala and Llanymddyfri (Llandovery), the present Konica Minolta Cup holders. There was a bar and a barbeque at the event which raised about £5,000.

Later that day a further £15,000 was raised at the promises auction. Among the items sold were holidays in Portugal, Tenerife and Malaga, a day's pheasant shooting which was worth £3,000 and a hospitality box for 12 people at the international between Wales and France at the Millennium Stadium, which alone raised £1,200.

By Christmas 2007 the fund had reached over £100,000

with contributions from many who had participated in the London marathon, events organised by clubs, schools, societies, sheepdog trials, WA Bala, concerts, quizzes, panel games and so forth. People from all parts of the country showed a great deal of initiative and originality in the range of events they organised.

All this activity exemplified the respect people had for Yogi and reflected the goodwill that is ever present in our community.

We are forever grateful that this is where we live.

CHAPTER 7

Half Time

i

THE PERIOD BETWEEN August and Christmas proved to be a very busy one for my family and my friends and all the kind people involved in money raising events. And it was a very important period for me in hospital, as well.

At the end of August and beginning of September Dilwyn Morgan went on his bicycle journey from Land's End to John O'Groats, and soon afterwards I started on a marathon as well, a different marathon to Dilwyn's – involving the computer. I had never even switched on a computer prior to this, let alone used it, and everything had to be done with the mouth. Quite an ordeal and it took me ages to learn to press the start button before proceeding any further. I have decided that I will not use it for all kinds of things, only to send a few e-mails and to surf the internet. Sounds simple doesn't it, but I can assure you it's not!

But within a week I had managed to print out a message to send to Teleri and Ilan, and I did that without the help of my tutor who was English:

Teleri and Ilan this is my first go.

A fortnight later I managed to send this message to Susan:

Hello, Hitler. Got this far. You can now reach me by e-mail. Will practice more until I get 'perfect'. Guess who!!!

During October Catrin, a television producer, came to the hospital to film me for the S4C Welsh programme *O'r Galon* (From the Heart) and this is how she related her story on the Internet:

> ...The hospital kindly arranged for me to film Bryan having his physiotherapy and a session learning computer skills. I felt that that was enough and that asking him questions afterwards would be too much for him...
>
> I had a short conversation with him and suggested that we didn't do the interview then because I didn't want to tire him.
>
> 'O no,' said Bryan. 'Let's get it out of the way.'
>
> And that was how it was. We started at two o'clock and the therapist kicked us out at a quarter to five because she wanted to go home. I had a great interview with Bryan... and it was hard work for him because he had been on the bicycle for half an hour previously and then had done some typing before answering my questions. I had to pause every now and then and give him a drink of water... When you see the programme don't be disappointed if your name is not mentioned. I can assure you that Bryan named everyone in the Bala area, if not half of north Wales, but I will have to edit you out because I have recorded two hours of interviewing and the whole programme lasts only half an hour.
>
> He looked a bit tired after returning to the ward and I was worried that we had overdone it. And what worried Bryan? That I had a long journey home!
>
> The whole experience was great and made me feel how lucky I am in my work being able to create a programme like this one and spending time with such an incredible person and incredible family.

Before Christmas about 30 children from Bro Tryweryn, Parc and Llangwm (three schools in the Bala area) came to sing carols, but the staff would not allow them to go from ward to ward in the hospital, only to sing in one place. This was because they sang carols and there was a possibility that patients with different faiths would be offended. Many of the patients were extremely disappointed, especially those who were confined to their beds and couldn't come to listen to them. I couldn't understand what all the fuss was about. I offered to go round the beds and ask the patients if they wanted to come and hear the children sing. I have never been a religious person myself, never a chapel-goer. My grandfather attended Sunday school in Melin-y-Wig at one time, and would describe how things were in the old days, and would quote from the Bible, but he had fallen out with them long before I was born and never worshipped anywhere. And when Bob was killed on the tractor I kept asking why, and no one could answer me.

Those visitors who came to see me regularly were a source of great strength to me during this period between September and Christmas. One day Trefor Trow called in; he was from the Bala area originally but had lived in Liverpool for 35 years. He got his tickets for rugby international matches from the Bala club and he arranged with Tony Parry to meet him in the hospital one evening so that he could pay for them when he visited me.

Trefor came every Thursday evening after that, staying to chat for a couple of hours. It helped me to know that someone would be coming regularly. The first time he spoke English because he had married a Liverpool girl and hadn't spoken Welsh for many years. But when he came the second time I began to speak to him in Welsh, and within six weeks his Welsh was perfect. He still keeps in touch by phone and has visited me here in Bala.

About the same time members of the Southport Rugby Club came to know that I was in the hospital. How, I have no idea, but their trainer and the chairman and his wife came to see me and presented me with the club shirt. And somehow, through the rugby club, Mark Vine the manager of Ainsdale Golf Club learnt that I was in the hospital and he, his wife and children started coming to see me every fortnight. I am very grateful to these people for their kindness to a complete stranger.

The period around Christmas was a bad time. I was still getting spasms, some of them so bad that they kept me awake all night, and I would be in bed unable to do anything for days afterwards.

One day Mr Soni the consultant came to see me and said

that he was going to prescribe some medicine called baclophen for me. It had to be administered through the belly and he had devised a pump to get the stuff inside my body – not unlike an alarm clock made of titanium, about seven or eight centimetres wide and a couple of centimetres in thickness. He went on worldwide tours to exhibit this particular contraption.

Fixing the machine entailed a four-hour operation: placing the machine itself and then a pipe to my belly and up my back to my shoulders. The big day was 22 December. He had come by a week earlier to ask if I was ready to receive the treatment, and I had told him that I was ready to try anything if there was the remotest chance that it would improve my condition.

Mr Soni conducted three of these operations at the same time, moving from one theatre to the next and instructing two other doctors, Dr Oo and Dr Anthony how to go about it so that they could conduct the same operation in his absence. It took all of four and a half hours and as a result I was in bed for three weeks, hardly moving, and on a special air bed which swivelled from side to side and up and down.

Because I couldn't raise my head, a mirror was fixed above my head so that I could watch television.

I told Susan and the children not to come to see me over Christmas but nevertheless they came on Christmas Day. The last thing I wanted was Christmas dinner, but they couldn't keep away and so I had to make the effort.

The period between Christmas and the New Year was also a very bad period. I had terrible pains as the effect of tablets and injections wore off and the pump started pumping the baclophen into my body at the rate of 300 millilitres to begin with, gradually increasing as the whole operation was controlled by computer. If anyone had asked me how much pain I had on a scale of one to ten, I would have said 20. That is how bad it was. Tears kept pouring down my face and if I had been in possession of a gun, I would have used it!

The nurses could do nothing to relieve the pain, because I was not to be moved, but their care was magnificent. On

Christmas night, after Susan and the children had gone home, Nurse Kelly, a red-headed nurse, stayed with me all night holding my hand and talking. During this bad time many other nurses did the same thing at various times including Nurse Helen. She had a husband and nine-year-old twins at home and when I said 'What are you doing here? You should be at home with your family,' she replied, 'I had Christmas Day at home, and that's all I needed.'

Yes, it was a bad time, but I learnt what devotion and care by the staff meant, devotion which went far beyond the call of duty, and with their help I pulled through.

ii

When I changed from playing football to playing rugby I was struck by the difference in camaraderie between the two games. After a game of football, everyone would go his own way or gather in small cliques of friends. But in rugby, things were completely different. Everyone was part of a close-knit community, no cliques, no small groups coming together – we were all as one, and we were all friends. The same feeling of everyone getting along together and socialising was there after training sessions as well, and I enjoyed training very much. In fact, I got more pleasure from training than I did from actually playing the game. Training with the rest of the squad, of course, but also on my own.

When I was playing football the only thing I had on the farm was a ball hanging by a rope from a roof beam in the barn, and I would jump up to head it every time I passed. But rugby required more practice, especially as I didn't have the faintest idea how to tackle. Luckily, I was strong, so I filled a sack with oats and hung it in the cowshed. I would tackle it every time I passed, laying into it and wrapping my arms around it. I also put a piece of leather underneath a hundredweight, placed it on my head or neck and raised it. The third part of training on the farm was to carry a massive tractor tyre up and down the yard at quiet times such as Sunday afternoons. I probably looked ridiculous to any onlooker, but these efforts strengthened my body, and I knew that the other lads in the club were also at it in their own individual ways.

I started playing rugby for the first time in the 1980s, and I was in the first team from the very beginning, playing against teams such as Pwllheli and Blaenau Ffestiniog, and getting soundly beaten by them. We would also play against smaller teams – Harlech and Porthmadog – and usually won those matches. When we joined the North Wales League, we would have trips down south to play in competitions such as the Brewers' Cup, at the level of Cardiff's third team. Rugby was an amateur game at that time.

And that's how things were for two or three years, the only change in my life being that rugby had replaced football, although not completely. Some of the lads formed another football team in Cerrigydrudion and I would occasionally play for them.

Then, in 1984, Glasebrook, the owner of Botegir died and, as a result, my life changed completely. Mam still lived in one of Glasebrook's rented houses and I had the option to buy it, a purchase that would safeguard Mam's future. I went to see a lawyer in Denbigh and learnt from her that the process of selling the property would take at least 18 months. A year and a half then for me to find sufficient money in order to buy the house, which is what I did, saving until the last minute before paying for it. I was still at Botegir during this time. I was keen to buy the farm, if I possibly could, as farming meant everything to me. And during all this time, I continued to play rugby for Bala and football for Cerrig.

I formed a business plan, took it to the Midland Bank in Corwen to request a loan and the bank agreed that I could spend up to £350,000 to buy the farm. This was a large sum at that time, but the bank knew how much the farm was worth, and I was confident that it would be enough to buy when it was offered on auction. But I was disappointed. The bidding took it to £375,000 and I could never raise the £25,000 extra that was needed.

Botegir was bought by the owner of Agri Electrics, a shop in

St Asaph – a man called Mr Smith. He also bought Plas Newydd, between Rhewl and Llandyrnog. He sold the business and the premises in St Asaph in order to buy the two.

I stayed at Botegir until 1987 before moving, at the age of 30, to 17 Maes Aled, Cerrigydrudion, although I was asked to stay on at the farm. But I was heartbroken because I had failed in my bid to buy it. Haydn and I received a generous redundancy payment but Taid didn't receive a penny, although he had worked on the farm for over 50 years. He was over 65, and so officially retired and on his pension, even though he was still working. This upset me greatly.

Glyn Doctor and his wife had bought a council house in Cerrig, but relations between them were strained and he wanted to sell. We bought the house with the redundancy money and Taid's contribution and the three of us went to live there. Mam had her own home as the house she lived in belonged to me, and the council paid her rent of £35 per week directly to me, as it was a better financial arrangement for them than finding another house for her. So, with Mam settled, I had to fend for myself and move the three of us to Cerrig. Haydn didn't drive and Taid wasn't fit to be behind the wheel of a car, so I moved everything from Botegir in a Cortina and a small trailer, making numerous journeys until, little by little, I'd shifted all that we needed. There was no room in a council house for half the furniture that was in Botegir, so we had to sell most of it. Taid chose what he wanted and the things he thought Nain would have kept.

The furniture included three large dressers and they were bought, together with many other pieces of furniture, by a buyer from America. On reflection, the price we got for the furniture was much too low, and we lost a fortune. But I managed to keep one of Nain's china tea sets that Taid had bought for her in Bala fair. It isn't worth much today, but it's the only thing I have to remember Nain. I was in charge of the farm until it was sold to Smith, and then for a further few months following the purchase arranging, amongst other things, for the sheep to be sold. And during this period I played football for Cerrig and rugby for Bala.

After moving to Maes Aled I had no difficulty in finding work. Eifion Evans, a self-employed businessman lived on the same estate and he had many working for him. He tendered for the job of clearing sections of the Clocaenog Forest for the Forestry Commission, felling the trees, sawing them into props and poles and stacking them prior to their being taken away. He called at my house to offer me a job, and so I became a self-employed woodcutter – an extremely dangerous job, a pretty boring one too, but one that paid well as I was given £22 per ton for cutting the trees and stacking them by the side of the road. The Forestry Commission would then take them away in huge lorries, to be sold for industrial purposes.

The biggest shock was the switch from being employed to being self-employed. At Botegir, there were no taxes for me to pay, no electricity or phone bills, everything was free and the wages relatively small. Now, I was much better paid but had to foot all the bills. Freebies were a thing of the past. Money had to be budgeted in a different way. Taid didn't work after moving to Cerrig, and Haydn only got occasional work on farms, so most of the responsibilities fell on my shoulders again.

Most of the workers began working between half past seven and eight in the morning, but as I was used to getting up early, I would get up about five, start work early and then finish at five like everyone else. During my first week I earned £300 which was a lot of money back then and quite a shock to the system. The largest sum I earned in a week was £870, but that was a long and hard week. About five or six of us worked on the Llanfihangel side of the forest and a similar number on the Cyffylliog side, and we would play silly tricks on each other, such as moving and hiding tractors. Childish really, but it broke the monotony.

Starting so early in the morning and being alone in the forest was against the rules of the Forestry Commission, but they didn't find out about it, and at about half past seven every morning,

Eifion would come to where I was working and toot his horn and check that everything was in order.

The work involved complete clearance – the large trunks going to industry for construction purposes, the smaller branches sold as poles, whilst the rest of the stuff went to a large factory in Chirk to produce chipboard. It was hard work but I was strong and healthy and I had enough energy to work at Llaethwryd farm in the evenings, helping with the haymaking and earning extra money for that as well. I was well acquainted with the family, friendly with John and Gerallt – father and son, and friends with Iwan Glasfryn who married Meinir, Gerallt's sister before taking over the farm.

Life settled into a regular pattern for the next two or three years, including working 'on the door' at The Bridge Hotel, Bontuchel on Friday evenings and at Maxine's, a club in Rhyl on Saturdays. After a while, I gave up the Friday shift at Bontuchel but carried on at Maxine's. That's where the country lads would come looking for girls, getting off every time not with girls from Deeside and Merseyside, but with local girls, girls from their own areas. I found that odd! But I had numerous opportunities to meet girls from other areas as I was working on the door, and could talk sensibly because I didn't drink whilst on duty. Nevertheless my English often sounded quite odd translating as I did from Welsh.

I got to know quite a few girls in this way and I would often meet them on Wednesday nights in Queensferry and Hawarden and similar places. There was a lot of fun to be had in those days. Then, suddenly, towards the end of 1988, I stopped working at Maxine's as well.

The club had two floors: the lower floor for the disco and dancing, and the upper floor which was quieter, where patrons had an opportunity to socialise. One night, I was on duty at the top of the stairs when I saw the light flashing behind the bar, a signal that there was trouble downstairs. So down I went and there was an almighty fight there. I got in amongst the participants and managed with the bouncers to throw two or three of them out of the club. But suddenly I realised that my shirt was wet and when I looked down I saw that it was soaked in blood. There was a cut in the flesh under my ribs and it was then that I remembered feeling something stinging my side whilst grappling with those who were causing the trouble. Someone had used a knife or a razorblade to attack me.

Luckily, the wound wasn't deep, but I decided there and then to quit. I had never experienced anything like this before, and besides, new rules were being introduced which meant that I would have to apply for a licence to work at the club.

But before leaving I had a party sometime before Christmas, with the other bouncers – a party that lasted most of the night and I got home around five. Soon after seven, I was on my way to work in the woods and, as I was travelling through Llanfihangel, and taking the turn towards Bodwen farm and the forest, a police car emerged from behind the shop and came after me, and I still believe to this day that it was waiting for me – what else would he be doing in Llanfihangel at that time of day?

I knew that I was over the limit and that I would lose my licence if I was caught, so there was nothing to do but put my foot down and race towards the site in the forest where I worked. I realised that the policeman would phone from his car for reinforcements to come to meet me, but I knew all the narrow roads of the forest like the back of my hand, having used them so often over the years. It was a race through the woods after that, and a few of the workers were standing at the side of the road, talking, when they saw me coming towards them with the police car behind me, its lights flashing. I did a handbrake turn and sped up another road, and the policeman tried to do the same, but he skidded into the ditch!

By the time he managed to free his car I had disappeared, and having reached the site where I worked I quickly parked the car. I could hear the policeman shouting and threatening, but he had no chance of finding me in the middle of the forest. I got a lift from there in one of the workers' vans and then went into hiding for three days, phoning home to let Taid know that I was alright.

But, of course, the police knew who I was after obtaining the number of the car, and they called at the house several times during those three days, looking for me, with Taid truthfully admitting that he didn't know where I was.

Finally I had to come home and face the music. Six months later I was summoned to court was given a £100 fine and three points on my licence for failing to stop when requested to do so by the police. But that was much better than losing my licence!

Working, training, drinking, dating the girls, playing rugby and some football; working hard and playing hard, that was life for me in the 1980s. And then I met Susan.

iii

Yogi had more visitors than any of the other patients in the unit in Southport and I and the family are extremely grateful to everyone who went to see him, and especially those who continued to do so week after week. Naturally, as time went on, the numbers decreased and towards the end of September, being dead tired myself, this is how I reacted in my website diary:

No one went to see Yogi on Tuesday, this worries me more than him.

Some people ask: 'How is Yogi?' and I always answer: 'the same as usual – he's very positive.' And sometimes the only response is: 'Remember me to him.' Then I say: 'why don't you go to see him?' And more often than not the answer is: 'Busy at the moment, I'll go when things have quietened down a bit.'

Well, this may come as a shock to some of you, but I'm very busy too, I'm a wife and mother and the only one earning at the moment; I ferry the children from one activity to the next, I visit Yogi in Southport four times a week, usually on my own, I pay the bills, make sure our clothes are washed and ironed, that there is food in the cupboards and on the table, that the house is fairly clean, and oh yes, I work as well, and that's only listing some of the things I do. For six days a week I'm a single mother. Busy? Very busy. Tired? Dead tired. Anxious? About everything – and the rest.

People had constantly warned me that, as time went by, the number of visitors would fall off, but as usual I didn't take much notice of what they said. In spite of this quite a few have been very loyal to Yogi from the beginning, making that long tedious journey once a week or once a fortnight and I'm very grateful to you all. I'm not very keen on the journey myself but I have no choice in the matter, I have to go, but more than that, I want to go. There are days when I wish I could lock the door and forget everything, but that's not an option for me.

The entry is dated 27 September, but three days later my jottings were more positive and my humour restored:

Haven't written for some days… nothing much to say… and no patience… so I must apologise. Dad lost his mobile phone… Mam found it in a saucepan… the phone, not Dad!

And this is the rest of the message:

I've been feeling a bit low recently… but I've given myself a good shaking and I'm back on track. Finding it hard at the moment… people moving on with their lives… while I'm at a standstill. No change in Yogi's condition… no change on the planning front… the house exactly as it was five months ago. Everyone enquiring about Yogi… but me… I just want to forget and ignore everything… feel as if I'm carrying the whole world on my shoulders.

On Friday I had a chance to close the door on everyone… a whole day to myself… I did a lot of thinking… and believe it or not… I feel a lot better. Ready to face everyone and everything once again.

Then again during Yogi's long stay in hospital there were also many things happening that raised my spirits and helped me to cope from day to day. One of these was Dilwyn's (Porc) cycle journey from Land's End to John O'Groats.

Dilwyn and Nia, with the bike on board a camper van, left Bala on 25 August intending to start from Land's End on the Sunday morning and reach Southport to visit Yogi on the Thursday after a five-day ride.

Things didn't begin well. Two minutes into the journey he was back where he started having cycled straight back to the parking ground! Then things got better and he cycled over a 100 miles to reach Okehampton on the first day, and 95 to reach Clevedon on the second – over 200 miles in two days, eight hours in the saddle on the first and seven on the second day. Another six hours of cycling on the third day and he was well beyond Leominster.

And this wasn't all he did – he phoned Yogi, talked to Welsh presenter Jonsi on the radio and was filmed as he cycled for the TV programme *O'r Galon*.

Thursday was a big day. I went to a caravan park near Chester to met Nia and Dilwyn. Also there were Catrin, who was filming for *O'r Galon*, and Alun Elidyr, her partner, who was to accompany Dilwyn to Southport.

We reached the hospital about two, just as Yogi was being shaved for the occasion. Unfortunately he hadn't had a good night but, nevertheless, he was in high spirits. He was dressed and taken in his chair to the day room to be reunited with Dilwyn – it was all very emotional until they began to compare each other's sores and started indulging in leg pulling as they always do.

The visit did a lot to raise Yogi's spirits and I availed myself of the opportunity to thank the staff for everything they were doing to cope with this sort of event.

By Saturday morning Dilwyn had reached Carlisle, and he crossed the Scottish border during the day and got as far as Crawford, hoping to arrive in Fort William on the Sunday. Unfortunately he had to circle Glasgow because a marathon to raise money for charities was being held in the city, and the heavy traffic he encountered resulted in his having to stay at Ardlui, near Loch Lomond.

As he was cycling towards Inverness an L E Jones lorry from Ruthin passed him, the driver tooting his horn in greeting. This spurred him on to pedal faster.

On my way to Southport on 5 September Nia phoned to say that Dilwyn had arrived in John O'Groats, having successfully completed the 900-mile journey.

His amazing effort raised over £10,000 for the fund and achieved a lot of publicity through his constant contact with radio programmes. Jonsi had been particularly loyal to him, being in touch every day.

Dilwyn's effort was unbelievable especially as he had to give up playing rugby because of an injury, and was actually waiting for hip replacement surgery.

The John O'Groats and Land's End Society nominated him for the Charlie Hankins Memorial Trophy. This was the man who had made the journey in a wheelchair, having lost his legs in the war in north Africa in 1943. The trophy is awarded to those who display fortitude and perseverance on a journey between the two places. Dilwyn is only the third person to receive this award. The other two are, by now, included in the *Guinness Book of Records*.

When Yogi is feeling low, the efforts of people like Dilwyn, as well as his own determination to overcome the accident, always seem to raise his spirits.

My own spirits during the period from August to Christmas seemed to swing from high to low; at times I felt confident that things were looking up and then something would happen to plunge me into despair again.

Towards mid October I received news that left me furious. When Yogi was in Intensive Care in Wrexham, I promised him that he would soon be home again, and I was determined to keep that promise. Things looked promising when we had the case conference with the local Health Authority, and we were quite confident that his care package would be arranged through an agency and that he would receive that care at home.

The shock came a few weeks before the work on the house was due to begin. The Health Authority reneged on their promise that Yogi would be cared for at home, and they suddenly decided to contact several care homes to see if they had the necessary facilities to look after him.

I was struck dumb and very angry. Hadn't we made it perfectly clear to the Authority that placing Yogi in a home was not an option? This is how I recorded my frustrations in my diary:

> I honestly feel like giving up, like burying my head in the sand – all this bureaucracy and prejudice. No one can put a price on family life. We are just an ordinary family, never been on benefits, never been out of work, the children have always done their best in all their activities. We've never put a foot wrong. We respect the law and pay our taxes without trying to hide anything.

Yogi wanted me to delay the building work until the Authority had made up their minds. But I disagreed with him. Yogi was coming home whatever the cost to us. I would never, never agree to his being placed in a nursing home. Everyone rallied around to support us and many of our friends were absolutely livid with the Authority.

Two days later I had a long chat with the person responsible for arranging Yogi's release from hospital, as a result the situation became clearer and I cooled down a bit!

I was told that nothing had been decided by the Health Authority and that the financial system was complicated – the medical and care aspects would be financed by the Health Authority, and the other half of the package, the equipment, would be paid for by the Health Wales Commission.

I was given to understand that an appropriate panel would decide on the case. But before the panel met, the Health Authority were legally bound to consider every option and that was why they had to contact care and nursing homes. They could have told me! It would have saved a lot of tears and heartache and frustration. Now that I knew, all I could do was await the panel's decision.

But during this period there were things that helped lift my spirits: they disconnected Yogi's breathing machine for two minutes and he remained pink; I managed to change the trachy without help, and I was able at long last to show him the final plans for the house. Six months after the accident he was moved from the Intensive Care Unit, although he would probably be back after the surgery to relieve the spasms. He had a spasm while I was changing the trachy – probably my fault.

I must mention the family meal we had on Saturday, 4 November. It was quite an occasion – the first time we had eaten a meal together for six whole months, except on Yogi's birthday. Yogi had a three-cheese pizza, something he'd fancied for ages, and because Rhun, Rhian Dafydd and Arwel from Parc had been to visit him there were plenty of delicacies on offer.

Yogi's moods were very unpredictable in the period leading up to Christmas; there were several bad spells when I had to ask people not to visit him, then when he was better asking them to visit again to help lift his spirits. The reason for all this was the spasms he suffered, so a few days before Christmas they decided to operate. Consequently he didn't want us to go to Southport on Christmas Day, he didn't expect us, but wild horses wouldn't have stopped us. Ilan, Teleri and I set off in the morning and he was so glad to see us. As he was flat on his back it wasn't easy to give him his Christmas dinner, but I managed somehow after chopping everything up. Luckily he doesn't like Christmas pudding, so I'd made him a trifle. I promised him a special celebration in 2008. He'd be home by then – I'd make darn sure of that!

CHAPTER 8

After the Interval

i

I WAS CONFINED to bed for three whole weeks after Christmas, the special bed which was turned every two hours.

During this time Mr Soni went to Switzerland, not to speak about baclophen but to introduce another device he had invented, the phrenic pacemaker, a device not unlike an ordinary pacemaker but one that could regulate breathing. Both parts of this new device were placed on the outside of the body, one under the ribs and the other on the chest, and a small battery, the size of a cigarette packet worked the device which delivered an electric shock to stimulate the lungs. I've had one test to see if my lungs have recovered enough for the device to be used on me, not so I'm afraid, but another test will be made within a year.

The two young doctors trained by Mr Soni cared for me in his absence, and it was they who monitored the pump that pumped the baclophen into my body. I had a bad time of it because I was still suffering terrible spasms in spite of the treatment I was receiving supposedly to stop them. At the same time my throat was troubling me with the hole growing bigger which meant a bigger trachy, starting with number seven and working up to number nine. Another complication was that the pipe kept blocking, and I was unable to breathe because my body was too weak to clear the phlegm.

Twelve hundred milligrams of baclophen was pumped into my body every day and in the same ward as myself was another patient receiving the same treatment but who was allowed to sit in his chair all day and only received 400 milligrams a day. He told me that the amount would be greatly reduced by the time he was ready to go home.

I had been moved from the Intensive Care Unit into the ward and I was fortunate enough to obtain a bed near the patio doors which opened out onto a small balcony. No one else fancied that bed because the wind and the rain could be troublesome. But I was overjoyed to get so much fresh air. And all the time baclophen was being pumped into me, and no one before had received such an enormous amount.

The nurses were most attentive and visitors kept coming to see me, but the spasms were as bad as ever. By the middle of May I had received over 2,200 milligrams of baclophen, enough to kill an elephant according to the doctors but the spasms were no better, and they couldn't understand why. Mr Soni returned from Switzerland but because he suffered from back trouble, he did not come back to the hospital for some time.

The pipe which entered my throat had been pinned to the bedclothes to keep it steady, and one day it blocked and the alarm went off. Two nurses rushed in at once and without pausing to think, one tugged at the blanket and the whole pipe came out tearing my throat and resulting in a larger pipe, ten millimetres in diameter having to be inserted. The hospital authorities made a great fuss over the incident and wanted to know who was responsible. They wanted me to make a statement naming the nurses, but I refused.

I had to be loyal to them; they had actually saved my life. I had started turning blue and their voices sounded to me as if they were far away in the distance. They had two options, to follow accepted procedure and do everything by the book which would have resulted in my death, or to do the right thing in the circumstances and thereby save my life, which is what they did. The authorities could find who was on duty anyway without my telling them. They only had to check the records, but they wanted me to accuse the nurses so that they could be disciplined, but I would never complain about the staff; I depended on them completely, and they were so good to me.

By now, a year on from the accident, I understood my body requirements and realised fully that I had to depend on the nurses for my toilet needs. I even got used to this eventually, and since I was so cheeky and seemingly unconcerned about it, the Sister decided that I was a good patient for trainees to practice on, although some were shy and never came near. I would indulge in some leg-pulling and help them to forget themselves.

Sister knew who to send and who not to, and those who came had to do everything for me. They had no choice. Sister and staff nurse left them to it but were never far away, administering to the needs of the patient in the next bed whilst at the same time listening to all that was going on by my bed.

You never learn by standing and watching, the only way is to have a go, that's what I believe anyway, and the more I could help them the better for them. I would tell the students that they had no choice; you have to take me to the toilet and clean me afterwards. And the more experience they had, the easier it became for them. I tried to help all the nurses in Southport whilst I was there because they were so good to me.

One day I had an MRI scan and, because I had a ventilator, the whole process proved much more difficult than was usual. Dr Watts and Sue Perrie Davies made all the arrangements and then I was moved slowly through the tunnel with a frame about my head to keep it still. I had to make sure that I wasn't wearing anything metal. Sue Perrie Davies came with me right to the edge of the scanner to ensure that everything was right, and the next moment there was an almighty bang and she was stuck in the machine. What had happened was that she was wearing an under wired bra and the magnet had got hold of it and held her by her bra. It was a most entertaining episode!

Then, on with the process guiding the breathing pipe into the scanner, a procedure which caused a noise like a pneumatic drill.

The scanner moved every 20 seconds and then stopped with the noise changing as it viewed different parts of the body, the head, back, arms and so on. The object of the exercise was to see if the backbone had recovered or deteriorated and whether the bones in the throat had changed in any way. In fact I think they were looking for my brain as well, and were unable to find it!

Towards the end of May, Mr Soni returned and there was a lot of work awaiting him. I told him that the spasms were as bad as ever, and he went to check the records. He came back and told me that it was a miracle I was still alive since no one had previously received more than 1,200 milligrams. He gave me a baclophen injection in the back and then told the nurses to take me out onto the pavement and bounce me up and down. They did this and I didn't have a spasm all day. I felt perfect.

Then he ordered an X-ray because he had no idea what had happened. He stuck a four-inch needle in my belly and into the pump and looked at the scanner to see what was happening. And he saw immediately that the needle was bent inside the pump.

He pulled the needle out and said 'You're back on the slab on Friday,' and that's all. But he came by on Thursday night and explained that the pump was pumping the baclophen correctly but because the needle was bent it wasn't being directed to the right place, and so it was totally ineffective. Thank goodness for that, otherwise I'd be dead! No, on second thoughts, if it had been effective I wouldn't have been given so much.

On Friday he put another pump inside me saying 'you're only a guinea pig'. That was fine, because one of the first things he'd asked me when he came to see me in Wrexham was whether I was prepared to be a guinea pig or not, and I had nodded my head.

I didn't relish the idea of lying on my back for three weeks after this treatment. I had recovered well after the last treatment and thought maybe that I was tougher than I actually was. But I was better this time although I had to lie still for three weeks, and this in spite of the fact that I felt fine and tried to persuade the nurses to raise me up, but, 'whatever Soni says we do' was the answer every time.

I had warned my friends not to visit me during this time thinking that I would be ill as before. But I was much better and the pump was working. When I came out of the theatre the staff woke me up and kept me awake for three days. Because so much baclophen had escaped from the pump into my system, there was a danger that I could sink into a coma and never wake up again. So the nurses sat with me all day and all night talking incessantly to keep me awake. And that is when I realised how hard nurses work. But they were successful because I am still here! And still talking!

ii

I am nine years older than Susan, so I remember her as a small child in Cerrig; indeed I more or less knew her since she was a little baby as I would go shopping to Cerrig with Nain, to Mrs Jones' shop, across the road from where Susan lived. Her father, Dic, was a policeman in Cerrig in those days, but he was long gone before I started driving and going to pubs. He was moved to Llandyrnog and then to Caernarfon.

When she was 18, and I was 27, Susan was engaged for a time to Rhys Derwydd, who lived on the farm across the river from Botegir, so I saw her from time to time when she visited the farm or went to the Crown in Llanfihangel. Because I fancied her then, I asked her to come out with me, but she ignored me, and that's how it was until she herself became a policewoman posted to the same station as the one her father had been in.

Girls would often be the topic of conversation for us rugby lads, and a fair amount of leg pulling went on. I admitted to them that I had fancied Susan for years and told them how she had ignored me when I asked her out. One night in early September, after the training session, the subject once again was girls and they dared me to go to Susan's house and ask for a cup of coffee.

I was never one to refuse a challenge, so I agreed to go, and so one night after training, and still wearing my rugby kit, I stopped the car in Cerrig and crossed the road to her house. When she came to the door I said: "Listen, don't look now but two or three of the lads are hiding behind the hedge over there and they've dared me to come here and ask for a cup of coffee."

"You'd better come in then," she said, and in I went.

Her cousin was there that night, and we had a cup of coffee, a biscuit and a chat – the first time we had ever talked properly. I don't know what happened to the lads but it was past midnight when I left, after turning to her on the doorstep and kissing her on the cheek before running away like a frightened schoolboy!

And that's when we started seeing each other, secretly for the first couple of months because I didn't want the lads to find out, otherwise I wouldn't hear the end of it. Me, of all people, with my chequered history going out with a policewoman! But after the first few weeks we decided we could come clean about it and so one evening we went together to the Crown in Llanfihangel, and when I walked in with her, the whole place went quiet, you could have heard a pin drop, and I could almost feel the staring eyes drilling into my back.

The night passed quite pleasantly, but as time passed by and I continued with my after hours drinking in the local pubs, I had to be careful, because when she was on duty she'd call in the pubs after stop tap to see who was there, and all she would see of me would be my shadow disappearing out of the back door as she came in through the front.

She knew perfectly well what was going on. When I had been training with the rugby team in Bala and returning home late, she would park by the garage in Cerrig, and flash her lights on me. Some of the girls living in the village said to her, 'there'll be no future for you whilst you're with him' as my reputation had arrived there before me. The Queens was run by the Glan Gors daughters and Susan was very friendly with them. But I learnt pretty quickly who were my friends and who were not. Before I started going out with Susan I would get told about everything that happened in Cerrig and Bala, who were up to no good and what they were doing, all the scandal, but from then on there were some who wouldn't tell me anything, even though they knew me well and knew that I would never grass on them to Susan.

My co-workers in the forest soon learnt that I was going out with a policewoman, in spite of the fact that I had been racing with the police and at times leading them a merry dance. I was the owner of a brownish-yellow Cortina at the time and, one afternoon, they sprayed the words 'Yogi loves PC Sue' in bright pink fluorescent paint on the bonnet, the roof and the doors on either side. I continued to drive that car for three or four months after that, but the paint never wore off!

But that's exactly the kind of thing I would have done to them. Yes, the old wheel keeps on turning, doesn't it, and the chicks keep on coming home to roost.

By now everyone knew about my relationship with Susan, and one night when I went to the Queens in Cerrig the whole place was in darkness, and I couldn't understand what was wrong. Suddenly, a flashing blue light lit the place up; some of the lads had stolen red lamps from the council and painted them blue. I had to suffer many pranks of that nature during the first few months of my relationship with Susan.

When Christmas came I brought Susan a tree, one that I had cut down in the night, and then carried on the roof of the car. But it was much too big; it reached right up to the ceiling!

In January, we started discussing engagement and marriage. We both lived in Cerrig, me in Maes Aled and Susan in the police station. But before getting engaged, I had to meet her parents – Dic and Morfudd – and we were both invited to Sunday lunch in Caernarfon. As it happened, I managed to get two black eyes playing rugby the previous day, as well as injuring my leg, so I looked like a limping panda.

But I got a warm welcome from the two and there was no lull in the conversation because Dic had been a policeman in Cerrig and in Llandyrnog, and I was acquainted with Prion where Morfudd was brought up, and knew her brother who worked for the Water Board. And the fact that Dic was an ardent Man U fan helped things, too. They welcomed me with open arms, and I got along better with them than with my own family. I told Mam that I was going out with Susan but not a word to the rest of my family until we got engaged.

I'm a tight one with money, as everyone keeps reminding me, so January was a good time to get engaged as I was able to buy a ring in the sales, and that's what I did, in H Samuels, Wrexham. But before that we had to tell Dic and Morfudd, and they were invited to supper at the police station in Cerrig. I asked Dic, in front of Morfudd, if I could marry Susan – yes, I formally asked for her hand. The answer I got was this: 'If you're foolish enough to take her, you're welcome to have her.'

After that, I told Taid and he was very glad because I was, by then, in my thirties. 'It's time for someone to get hold of you and sort you out,' were his words, and fortunately he and Susan understood each other and got on well from the start.

Susan knew that I would never turn my back on Taid as he had done so much for me, so there was no intention of marrying straight away after getting engaged. In a year or two, maybe, but certainly not sooner.

iii

The year 2008 began with a meeting in Plas Coch to discuss all the necessary changes to the house. Yogi couldn't come home until the alterations had been completed, so it was all hands on deck as soon as possible.

Yogi was in a bad way after the operation and the spasms were no better. He was fine while we were there on New Year's Day, but he'd suffered a massive one the night before. Nevertheless he was in a good mood and enjoyed his beef dinner. Ilan fed him saying it was pay-back time for feeding him when he was little, and he used the same procedure – 'a spoonful for me, a spoonful for you!'

All the patients were in good spirits and the doctors and staff had been wonderful. By now Yogi was allowed to sit up at an angle of 20 degrees, and the slightest development was good for morale.

The work on the extension to the house began on 5 January. A local builder, Paul Morgan, was responsible for the whole project and the first job was to clear the ground and lay the foundations. There was plenty of help at hand and volunteers started arriving before I set out for Southport – El and Megi Tŷ Nant, Ynyr Aeddren, Dewi Disgarth and Eryl Vaughan. Several others turned up and I can only guess who they were from Mam's description of them. So all I can do is to thank everyone who came that day. Yogi was very grateful and greatly impressed with the goings on.

By mid January he was much better and ready to receive visitors again. He enjoyed seeing pictures of the workers around the house, and commented that there was too much tea drinking going on!

On 15 January, *O'r Galon*, the S4C programme that Catrin had worked on so hard for months was shown on television. It was a good programme and the response has been unbelievable.

The events held to raise money for the fund were going from strength to strength, some in the most unlikely places. I went to a farewell do in Wrexham for Inspector Arfon Jones, and his wife decided to organise a raffle, another guest decided to make a collection and raised £300. At the same event another friend and colleague, Helen Lloyd Jones, gave me a cheque for £100, the proceeds from the auctioning of a signed shirt.

Towards the middle of February Ilan, Teleri and I attended an important event at Plas Coch. The hoteliers, Aled and Edwina, had arranged an evening of light entertainment with Glesni Fflur, Edwina's daughter who was a singer and had come especially from London; Farmer Ffowc a local comedian, and a popular singer Geraint Roberts together with his band, with Dilwyn Morgan of course as compere. Believe it or not £2,000 was raised that night.

I mention these as an example of the variety of events that were arranged to boost the fund and we cannot thank people enough for their amazing kindness. They not only boosted the fund but raised our morale as well.

Towards the end of January I was allowed to take Yogi in a wheelchair to the day room, after checking that I had all the paraphernalia with me – the ambi bag, the spare trachy and the suction pump. It was a first time on my own with him, and it was rather like taking Ilan out for the first time when he was a baby. But this was only an interim arrangement; pretty soon he would have a wheelchair which he could control himself.

Another landmark in February was when the three of us stayed in a hotel in Southport for three nights and Mam and Dad joined us with one of Arvonia's trips (a bus company from Gwynedd). Yogi was allowed to join us for dinner at the Richmond, his first time out of hospital since his accident. A nurse had to accompany him of course and Jeannette came although it was her day off. The dedication of the staff never ceased to amaze me.

Unfortunately the day was not without its mishap because Teleri caught her finger in the car door and I had to take her to Alder Hay Hospital in Liverpool the following day. She was assessed and then we had to wait all day for treatment because there was an emergency which took priority. Eventually at four o'clock in the afternoon we were told to go back to Southport and return at eight the following morning. It was quite a serious injury. She had broken her finger and badly bruised the root of the nail. She was in the theatre by nine o'clock the next day and ready to go home by a quarter past ten. We were to return to Alder Hay in a week's time to have the stitches removed.

The object of our three-day stay in Southport was to save me from too much driving! These sort of accidents happen to people all the time of course, but when the mainstay of the family is flat on his back in hospital everything seems to be more of a burden.

Before the end of February I met a representative of the Health Board to discuss what equipment was needed for Yogi's homecoming. The meeting went well and I felt that things were improving. By now Yogi was in his new wheelchair and beginning to get the hang of the chin control. Then something went wrong with the chair and he had to do without it for six whole weeks.

This year I had to go to the preliminary stages of the Urdd (Welsh League of Youth) Eisteddfod with Teleri. It used to be one of Yogi's responsibilities, and then I would go to the actual Eisteddfod while he played rugby. This was another of Yogi's duties falling on my shoulders, but Teleri did well, she won second place in the harp solo and third for her singing, years 5 and 6.

A week later Ilan had a big problem. He was offered a ticket to see his favourite team, Man U, play at Old Trafford, but he was also looking forward to going to Southport to see his dad. So he phoned Yogi to ask his opinion. I already knew what the answer would be; Yogi always considered everyone else before himself. So Ilan went to Manchester with a clear conscience, and the team lost!

Early in April I spent four nights with my friends and colleagues Sam, Gail, Petra, Helen and her daughter Ellis in Lanzarote. We had a wonderful time although it was hard being so far from home, but I phoned the hospital every day and texted the children regularly.

The procedure Yogi had undergone before Christmas to stop the spasms hadn't worked and it was likely that it would have to be repeated.

Another of Mr Soni's innovations was one which would regulate the air in his lungs. Yogi was tested to see if he was a suitable candidate for the treatment, but unfortunately the tests proved to be negative and Yogi was very, very disappointed.

But his spirits rose again when his electric chair came back and he was like a child with a new toy. I won't repeat the saga of the split pipe when we went walkabout in the hospital with Alwyn Ambulance, only to say that Yogi and a speedy wheelchair is a very dangerous combination and not good for my blood pressure.

This is what I wrote on the website on Saturday, 19 April 2008, exactly a year since the accident:

> A year ago today, Yogi took Ilan to Wrexham to play football. He came home, changed and went down to the rugby club to play in his last game against Nant Conwy. I remember the day as if it were yesterday. I can see Yogi leaving 'Tŷ Ni' saying he would be late back because

131

he wanted to go to Llanuwchllyn to see Osian who had been injured playing rugby the night before.

Our lives changed for ever on that day, who would have thought then that we would still be waiting for Yogi to come home.

Yes, today is very difficult for me, emotionally more than anything. Yes, I still cry now and then, time doesn't heal the pain. Yes, we have come to terms with the situation, but nothing will ever be the same again, for Ilan, for Tels, for all of us.

I would like to thank everyone for all the support, the help, the fundraising and more than anything the many, many visits to Walton, to Wrexham and to Southport.

But the house was coming along well and we were confident that Yogi would be home by August. Our target was the 27th – his birthday. Another piece of good news was that the Wales Heath Commission had agreed to finance his treatment. And better still, the second procedure to get rid of the spasms had been successful, and hopefully they had been cured once and for all.

CHAPTER 9

Open Territory

i

HAVING BEEN KEPT awake for three days because of the amount of baclophen in my system, things started getting better, although my throat kept giving me trouble. But I didn't have to return to the Intensive Care Unit this time, I was allowed to stay in the ward, and that was an encouraging sign. The second treatment made a great difference to the spasms, and the dosage was reduced from 2,000 milligrams to under 500.

In three weeks' time I was sitting up in bed and receiving visitors again, but the next step was getting into the chair, and that was some step. Exactly as before I went out like a light because my blood pressure dropped so suddenly, and the nurses had to adjust the front of the chair pretty quickly to raise my feet as high as possible so that the blood would flow back to my head.

I came to gradually and expressed the wish that it was how I wanted to die if I had the choice, because it was such a nice feeling, being light-headed and painless as if I was on a cloud seeing the stars going round and round me. Everyone started laughing when they heard this, but I was serious about it.

It was a quiet period for me after that, gaining strength every day and going around the ward in the chair that had been loaned to me, visiting the other patients and making friends with them, telling them my story and listening to theirs.

Some of the things they had to relate were unbelievable. Gerry, for example, a pilot with British Airways, 6 feet 4 inches tall, and thin as a matchstick. He went swimming while on vacation in Mexico, and one day whilst standing in the water, a huge wave knocked him down and he broke his back in two places. He is like me now, unable to move from the neck down but, unlike me, he can breathe without assistance.

But the strangest tale was the one by the man from beyond Preston, I don't remember his name. He wasn't married but had taken a fancy to the woman next door. She had a little dog, and when she went on holiday he said that he would look after it. One day he went for a walk with the dog, tripped across the lead, fell, struck his head in the ground and broke his neck. But, unlike me, he broke it perfectly square near the second vertebrae and they managed to make good the break by using pins. He wore a frame in hospital for three months and then he walked out as if nothing had happened. I told him he should have jumped over the fence to get at the woman, and forget about the dog!

There were 40 of us in the ward and no two people had exactly the same injury.

I was gaining strength during this period and friends came to visit me during the week and Susan and the children at weekends when we could go out together. This was the period when Susan was learning to change the trachy, and after she became competent enough it was the turn of the children. Both of them can now perform the operation equally well.

During this period – around the beginning of August I think – having had lessons on the computer, my attention was drawn to a chair with a four-wheel drive advertised on a website, and the nurses printed the page for me. Some man from Telford was selling them and he was contacted and asked about these machines. He said that they cost £12,000 and came from Australia. He was importing them and selling them in Britain. So much money had been contributed to the fund, thanks to the kindness of everyone, that I decided to go for one and started the process of ordering.

But then the Health Board came into it and said that they would pay for the chair. I let the agent from Telford know about this and the money intended for the chair was spent as part of the cost of making alterations to the house.

Then the Health Board changed its mind and decided that they would not pay for it after all, and because the money earmarked for it had by now been spent on the house, I had a problem what to do, and spoke to the hospital authorities about it. They said that if the promise by the Health Board was made in black and white – and it was – that they would have to keep their word. The seller said that he would keep the order open for me until I had the money. And that was the start of a long period of wrangling with the Health Board which lasted for almost a year until the chair finally arrived. The whole story is in the *Daily Post* on 21 September 2009. Incredible!

In mid August the borrowed chair promised to me was delivered and I was given permission to go out of the ward in it in order to get accustomed to it. So, on the afternoon when Susan and Alwyn Ambulance came to see me we ventured to the canteen. But we went down the lift to begin with in order to go along the corridor at the bottom. I was determined to try it myself without any help and control it with my chin, using the chin control as it was called, and there was a pipe leading from my chin to the arm of the chair. I entered the corridor and drove myself along it, behaving like a child with a new toy, going like the clappers with people shouting after me because I was wobbling from side to side not being used to the chin control.

Then, back up to the canteen which was upstairs, so into the lift and then at the top I had to reverse out and, whilst manoeuvering, the pipe in the breathing apparatus got stuck in the door and broke in half. The alarm went off and I was gradually choking since I could only breathe out, whilst Susan was livid and in a panic.

The ambi bag was used quite quickly – the bag kept nearby to give me air should something happen to the pipe, the bag that keeps me alive in a crisis, and there could be no greater crisis than something happening to the ventilator which keeps me supplied with oxygen. Alwyn Ambulance got hold of the two broken pieces of pipe and held them together, and that is how I arrived back in the ward.

Susan was mad with rage and threatened that I would never be allowed in the chair again, whilst I could do nothing but smile foolishly at her. Sister Carol came in and I thought all hell would break loose when she heard the story from Susan, because I had acted foolishly and put my life in peril. But her reaction was completely different. She said that I was doing everything possible to get well and that I could go in my chair any time provided Susan or someone else was with me. If you managed to deal with the broken pipe she said, you can deal with anything.

There was no stopping me after that!

Many of the hospital staff helped me to get out as well and I shall be forever grateful to them.

One was Lucy Gough, a nurse who came in on her day off to take me out. Another one was Alison Smith – Smiler as we used to call her.

After I had got used to the chair we would go out on a Saturday for lunch to a small tavern not far from the hospital, and the children were forever telling me that they wanted to operate the ambi bag and fix it on me. They were practising one day in the hospital when Alison came in. She thought that they had been instructed how to do it by the hospital, but when she heard that they were self-taught she was very annoyed and said that she could lose her job if the authorities found out, because she would be blamed for letting it happen.

But that is how they learnt, and it was better that they learnt in the ward rather than outside. After this they felt more confident and I had confidence in them as well.

By September the search was on for a company which could provide carers to look after me when I got home, and the choice had to be made between five companies who tendered for the work. All the enquiring about what I needed and what was available and the offers from the different companies was beyond me, and I found it very difficult to decide anything. I said that I didn't know what to expect whilst they, of course, were initially offering me everything!

Sister Carol sat with me and explained what to expect, what

to accept and what not to. She knew the ropes and she said I would be lucky to receive half of what the companies promised. She also said that whoever got the contract would take three months to get used to me and that I would take a similar time to get used to them. And she was absolutely right.

In the end I left everything to Susan. The company that got the contract was Inclusive Lifestyle from Chester, and before they finally won it a consultant working for the company came to see me, one who obviously knew his job, knowing everything I wanted to know and answering all of my questions, and he said that he would probably be in charge of the service package. I talked to the other patients and consulted the nurses and they all thought that what I was being offered was good. But after the company got the work I never saw him again. Their contract came to an end on the last day of September 2009, thank heavens for that!

After that it was a quiet time with a few visitors breaking the monotony, such as Iwan Tan y Foel, and Elgan, Jack Arthur Jones' son, on their way from Carlisle where they had been selling bulls. There was no empty space in the car park, so they parked their lorry outside the front door and came in, in their working clothes covered in cow muck!

The nurses had never seen anything like it, and I told them that there were two bulls in the back of the lorry. They didn't believe me, so I asked Iwan to move his lorry round the corner and park it under the balcony, and all the nurses went to the window to have a look, and they were amazed, never having seen anything like it before.

They knew nothing about hard times in the countryside, but I would tell them about my escapades when they sat by my bed, some that are included in this book, and some that are not, for fear of finding myself in jail – which I almost did on more than one occasion!

By this time there was talk of my going home and people were starting to enquire when that would be. I was wise enough not to give heed to any promises, since I had heard other patients being told they would be home within the month and seeing them still there two months later. But things were slowly moving.

A young woman called Natasha came to see me; she would be controlling the contract and the staff on behalf of the company from Chester. They found, with Susan's help, six carers, and they came to see me and started to learn the job. I'm hopeless with names, so Susan got photos of all six for me, and I gave each one a nickname and in this way learnt to remember them.

One young woman, Sheryl, came from Wrexham and she was called 'Blondie', Kevin from Llanrwst was 'Baldy' because he had no hair, Kate from Corwen was 'Smilie', then there were Mair from Bala, Elfed from Ffestiniog and Julie from Corwen – 'the good, the bad and the ugly'! I hasten to add that Julie wasn't ugly; she was in fact a very pretty girl!

In September they came to Southport to be trained and Sister Carol was responsible for them. During this period of instruction two of them would work a day and night shift, following the same pattern as would be operated when I got home. They stayed in bed and breakfast houses in Southport alternately with going home. All six had some experience of dealing with disability, Julie and Sheryl worked with Inclusive, Mair had worked in the community in Bala, Elfed in a home in Ffestiniog, Kelvin was a fitness instructor in Betws y Coed, Kate was a cook in St David's College in Carrog.

I was the one who showed them how to change the trachy and clear the pipe, and all six came together to learn. My throat was a bit sore after this but we had a lot of fun and they all worked hard during the six weeks they were in Southport. The sooner they learnt their job the sooner I'd be home, and that would be the next important event in my life, the most important since the accident.

ii

Getting engaged in January, then marrying in a year or two, that was the plan to begin with, but when I realised sometime around April that Susan's birthday fell on a Saturday that year,

I suggested that we get married on that day, and she agreed. One of the main reasons I had for suggesting the date in the first place, and this is a fact, was to avoid having to buy two presents for her every year – birthday and wedding anniversary presents!

I had told her that I would never leave Taid and she was most understanding about that. In fact I wasn't really leaving him when I got married because the police station was almost opposite Maes Aled, convenient enough for me to tend to his needs, including making sure that he got his breakfast every morning.

Susan and I fell out a few times before the wedding day arrived, and no wonder as we were so alike, stubborn and unwilling to give in. I well remember one argument about something – I can't remember what – but I was pig-headed as usual and left the house to go to work while she was still angry. About nine o'clock, I noticed a car coming down the road through the forest towards where I was working. It was Susan – she'd come to apologize. I pretended not to see her and carried on working for about a quarter of an hour while she sat red faced in the car.

Finally, she got fed up of waiting for me to take notice of her and in her temper she tried to turn the car around to leave. The manoeuvre landed her in the ditch, and she couldn't move an inch. I went over to her then and laughed in her face raising the front of the car as she tried to drive it away. We got it from the ditch little by little, but she got the last laugh because the front wheel was spinning like mad, showering me with mud until I was covered from head to toe. Then we both started laughing and forgot why we'd been arguing in the first place.

Yes, we were both stubborn, the only difference being that she blew her top straight away while I was slow to lose my temper and slow to forgive. I go for weeks without losing my temper, but when I do, look out, it's amen after that!

As we had decided to get married on Susan's birthday, 25 August, we had to phone her parents straight away, because Susan had told them when we got engaged that we wouldn't set the date for a year or two. Morfudd was upset when she heard as she had planned to put in double-glazed windows in the house that year, and now the money would have to go towards the wedding. Dic, Susan's father, came on the phone to ask me if she was pregnant – it sounded like a shotgun wedding!

They couldn't really afford the wedding just then, having thought that they would have plenty of time to save towards the occasion, but they agreed in the end, fair play to them. From then on, I had nothing to do with the arrangements; I had only to 'turn up' on the day. Everything was done by Susan and her mother, and her parents were very supportive throughout.

The service was in Seilo Chapel, Caernarfon, and we were married by the minister, the Rev. Harri Parri. As I hadn't been baptized or confirmed the wedding cost me £70 – payment to the chapel for allowing us to get married there – and I've never let Susan forget that! But there weren't any problems with her because she was a member.

She went to Caernarfon three days before the wedding and stayed with her mother and father, whilst I travelled there on the day with my brother-in-law, Deio, who was my best man. He didn't drive so I was the chauffer for my own wedding, and I was so excited that we had to stop at a few pubs on the way.

Susan had arranged for someone to film the wedding on video, but all they saw of the two of us was me parking the car and then the two of us walking to the town as we had arrived early. But the video also showed Susan getting ready for the day, and it's a treasure worth having; it's so nice being able to look back.

We had to get back in time because I had threatened Susan that if she was more than five minutes late I was going to leave and not return! Karen Lewis, a friend of Susan's from the police was bridesmaid, and so was Lisa, the daughter of Russell and Jackie, another policeman and his wife who lived next door to us in Cerrig.

The sweat was streaming down my face and onto the end of my nose during the service and Harri Parri told the whole congregation that he had never seen anyone sweating so much in a wedding. But everything was fine and then we had the reception at Seiont Manor, a hotel in Llanrug. On my side of the family Mam was there along with my brother and sisters, a cousin from Coedpoeth and his family, and Taid. As Susan had a large family, I couldn't invite all my friends so we decided not to invite any of them in case we offended someone. I must admit that many of them didn't even know that I was getting married, as I'd tried to keep it a secret. I would never have got as far as Caernarfon had they known about it.

I arranged with Dr Owen, Cerrig, to book the small villa he owned in Ibiza for our honeymoon, but a fortnight before the wedding he came to me and said his daughter wanted the place at that time, so there was to be no Ibiza for us. I had never been overseas before and there wasn't much time to rearrange. There was nothing for it but go to the travel agents and ask where we could go for the money we'd already spent on the flight. In the end, we found ourselves in Tunisia. In my opinion, having being there, one of the worst places in the world for a honeymoon.

We arrived at breakfast time and had eggs that were fried so hard they were like leather. They would have stuck to the wall if I had placed them there. And if I'd thrown the sausage on the floor, it would have bounced back on the plate. The hotel was no good at all; there were no beds there, only mattresses with some concrete blocks under them, and anyway I spent most of the first three days in the toilet, being sick – the leather egg's fault probably. And Susan was ill later on in the week. She'd brought sun cream with her but had quickly used it all, so I went to buy her some more. I had no idea what I was buying but I got hold of something that looked like sun cream, which turned out to be oil, and in the hot sunshine, that was worse than nothing at all. Susan had sunstroke, and she got sunburnt so badly that she had to spend days on end in the shower trying to prevent her skin from blistering, and all she did was cry and ask for her mother!

We were there for ten days, and it was a terrible place. We

weren't allowed to put paper down the toilet; actually, they didn't use paper, only stones! There was no point in going from the hotel to the town because there were people – children in particular – begging everywhere, with many pursuing us trying to persuade us to buy this and that. Susan had dyed her hair blonde for the wedding and light hair was very popular in Tunisia. I was offered a hundred camels for her. I said at the time that I'd never go anywhere overseas after that. I haven't kept that promise, but it was five years before I ventured a second time.

iii

The messages on my website reflected my growing optimism that things were getting better; fewer negative things to moan about and many more positive messages about Yogi and the preparations for his return home.

On 18 June I was able to record that the second operation to relieve the spasms had been successful, and the daily dose of baclophen pumped into his body was greatly reduced. That was the good news. Not so good was the fact that his throat caused him a lot of discomfort, something that happened often, and still does.

On the same day I noted how well the building operations were developing. The builder, Paul Morgan, headed an excellent team: Nia, Pete, Stan, Raymond, Robin Wyn and Shelly were busy painting, Peter and Shane fitting doors and skirting, and Howard the plumber and the electrician Hywel were on schedule. The dream to get Yogi home for August was still a possible reality.

Before the end of the month I wrote about something that had happened on Friday, 13 June – not that I'm superstitious! In retrospect it was all quite funny, but at the time it was the sort of thing that once again underlined the importance of having a man about the place – Yogi would have dealt with it so much better than I did.

All that happened was that Teleri woke me at a quarter past seven one morning to say that a cow, some calves and some sheep had jumped the fence into our garden and then gone on to Alan next door's garden. I dashed out in my pyjamas to round them up and send them back into the field. But unfortunately, calves will be calves, and one of them dashed towards Alan's greenhouse smashing a lot of glass before careering headlong through Jaqui, Bill and Mandy's gardens. Fortunately, it didn't do much damage there and I offered to pay for repairing Alan's greenhouse. Of course he refused. But my cry was, 'please hurry home, Yogi, to sort us all out again'.

Yogi enjoyed hearing about all the ups and downs of our everyday lives at home and seeing pictures that I took of the developments in the house. But I often wasted our time together telling him about my work and all my worries and frustrations. He was always a good listener and I missed that as much as anything, but I was mad with myself for wasting our precious time together with my whingeing.

One of the major decisions I had to make before he could come home was what sort of vehicle to buy, one that would accommodate him and the wheelchair. Together we considered all sorts and of course he was keen to have a van that would take the children as well – ready for the time when he would be able to take them on rugby trips once again. He was so positive, and he won the day. As usual! The van was purchased by the Welsh Rugby Charitable Trust.

But not everything went our way and our greatest worry was the lack of carers. The firm promised a team of eight – that was the ideal number – but when they advertised at the beginning of July there were only two applicants. The dream of getting him home in time for his birthday in August was quickly receding and that meant a prolonged stay in hospital for him and more stress for me travelling back and forth to Southport.

The house wouldn't be ready anyway, although the team were making good progress. But absolutely everything would have to be finished before we could risk bringing him home.

The summer holidays came and Yogi suggested that the three of us should go to Tenerife for a week. Shortly before this the

Welsh Rugby Charitable Trust had sent some money to Yogi to pay for a holiday and he insisted that the children and I should spend it. That was Yogi all over. Anyway we went to Tenerife for a week's relaxation. But it was difficult to relax completely, being so far from home, and I felt anxious throughout our stay, although I kept in constant touch with the hospital. And it was an unfortunate experience for the children to see other fathers swimming and having fun with their families, and comparing our situation to theirs. But this was something we would have to get used to.

Once again my birthday and our wedding anniversary dawned, the second time with Yogi in hospital. We spent part of the day having lunch at the Richmond which was, by now, a sort of second home for us. Then the van arrived and I ventured to drive it to Southport. I felt as if I was driving a bus! The journey went well until I got to the parking lot outside the unit, where I managed to drive over the kerb. And who was it watching from the window? Who but Yogi! His first question to me was, 'Does that van have square wheels?'

And then on 3 September this is what I wrote:

> Well I am now able to say that Yogi won't be home until next month. Time drags for him in Southport, the days are long and the nights longer. Some days no one comes to see him, but he never complains. He was confined to bed for a few days but he's back in his chair again. The work on the house is nearly finished; there is some cleaning up to do and a few odds and ends to be seen to. But I hope the worst is over. There is still some painting and cleaning to be done and I'd like to appeal for a few volunteers. I know how busy you all are and I understand if you can't help. As ever, the week has rushed past. Tels started in secondary school and is enjoying it enormously so far. Ilan is still growing – 6 feet 3 inches by now and his new football boots are size 14. He's started calling me 'short-arse'. But he had quite a shock on Sunday when Siôn Goronwy called, he's much taller than Ilan and his feet are bigger than his!

Yogi was itching to come home and things were moving: the carers at the hospital being trained carefully by Carol, and the firm promising to recruit more – although that was questionable knowing the problems they'd had from the very beginning. But Yogi has recounted all this so I won't go over it again, only to say that the number of carers rose to six.

This is what I wrote at the end of October:

A week to go and Yogi will be home. We are so looking forward to it. Of course there will be a period of adjustment and settling down to a new regime for all of us. But we will take things one day at a time, and we will cope. Our priority this week is getting the house ready for the big day. A lot of cleaning and sorting things out, but with Mam's help we'll get it all done. I could never have managed without her. There's a lot yet to do but there's light at the end of the tunnel, and it's a very bright light!

CHAPTER 10

Crossing the Game Line

i

I HAD BEEN home once during my long stay in hospital, and that was on 8 May, over a year since my accident. It was Tony Parry (TP)'s fiftieth birthday and I was allowed to attend his party, about a fortnight before the second pump was installed in my belly.

Dr Watts and Nurse Lucy accompanied me and because the chair I had in hospital was so big, it wouldn't fit into the minibus, so I had to travel stretched out on my back. It was quite an ordeal and the journey took over three hours.

The news that I was to be home spread like wildfire around Bala, but somehow the information was kept from TP. I was driven to the door of Tŷ Ni but because I was flat on my back I couldn't really see the changes that had already been made to the house.

Then on to the golf club where the party was held and TP's face was an absolute picture when he saw me. It was important that I was there because he had been so loyal to me, coming to see me regularly, arranging visits by others, in touch with other clubs and those raising money for the fund. I stayed at the party for two hours and then it was back on the three-hour journey to Southport.

That was the longest period I had been out of bed – eight hours in all, and it took me well over a week to get over the journey and the visit. When Susan and the children came to see me at the weekend I told them that the next time I came home it would be for good. And that is what I told everyone who came to see me – home for ever, and no going back.

At long last that great day arrived and Margaret Maule and Sue Perrie Davies from the hospital arranged everything, moving all the equipment into the van and preparing for the journey. Getting me home was a major operation and that in the new van kindly donated by the Welsh Rugby Charitable Trust.

During the few days prior to my going home I dwelt in my own little world. So much had happened during the last fortnight, so many people coming to see me, so much coming and going that I was quite confused, not knowing exactly what was happening. And then I had to say goodbye to everyone, especially to the hospital staff, and that was the hardest task I had undertaken since burying my Taid and Nain. It tugged hard at my heartstrings; it had been such a long time and I had felt so secure in hospital. All the nurses who were off duty came to bid me farewell and one of the best things about the whole episode was all the kisses I received in one day!

It was Alwyn Ambulance, Ilan and Teleri who came to fetch me, and the first stop was outside the Plas Coch Hotel – my first home, according to Susan! Edwina and Aled the proprietors, together with some of the lads from the rugby club were out on the street waiting for me with a bottle of champagne and a huge banner on the front of the hotel which proclaimed – 'Croeso Adre' (Welcome Home). It was a fine dry November day.

Then on to the Cae Croes estate where I lived, and after turning from the main road I saw another big banner on the side of the road made by children from two local schools – Parc and Bro Tegid with the words 'Croeso adre i Yogi' (Welcome home Yogi) on it. There waiting for me were Susan, her parents Dic and Morfudd, and Sister Karen Smith from the High Dependency Unit in Bangor. She was responsible for everything at home because she worked for the Health Trust.

Kevin, one of the carers, was in charge of the wheelchair and when taking me out of the van he managed to upset Ilan and Teleri by taking me straight into the house. They had so looked forward to doing this and being the first to show me the new interior. Kevin really needed an 'L' or 'D' plates on the chair when he was pushing it; he struck my feet against the railings and bumped into the door and the sofa with the chair.

But there were so many changes made to the house that it didn't feel like home at all. People, not the building make a home I know, but it was such a strange place, there was an extension in front and at the back, the garage had disappeared and in its place a room built for the carers. It is hard to express it in words but I felt completely lost for a minute and tears were streaming down my face. Then I went into the kitchen and saw the stairs and thought of the countless times I had run up and down them, realising that it would never happen again.

That is when everything really struck me I think. I felt so empty, not knowing the place and yet people around me saying: 'You're alright now, you're home.' But I wasn't alright. Far from it.

The work that had been done on the house was unbelievable, and it was difficult for me to comprehend that people had worked so hard. I don't know what I expected, but somehow all the changes made were a great shock to me although I had known about them before coming home.

The bedroom was like a room in a palace; I had never imagined it would be such a big one. Then I saw the bed especially made and prepared for me. I had five minutes to myself there and facing me was a 50-inch television set looking back at me. This would probably be my best friend from now on. This is when it really dawned on me what the future held. It was so easy in hospital, looking forward to going home always kept me going. Over and over in my mind I kept asking – what's left for me? Will I be left with only a 50-inch television set to keep me company?

From that moment on I hardened my heart. In hospital everyone was so positive in their attitude, but here it was more difficult to look to the future. Most of the afternoon was lost in my mind, totally blank. I could hear the sound of chatting everywhere, people coming and going, people setting up the equipment, the sound of greetings and farewells.

In the evening, because it was 5 November, there were

fireworks in the field nearby whilst I sat in my bedroom gazing out and hearing from the patio the voices of parents and children talking, together with the members of the rugby club who had come to celebrate. I don't think I have ever cried so much as I did that day, but I couldn't even wipe away my own tears. It was a very special time of course, a day full of emotion, with everybody wishing me well, everybody doing their best, and I myself, feeling so empty and desolate inside.

ii

After the marriage ceremony in Seilo, a reception at Seiont Manor and a honeymoon in Tunisia, we made our home in the police station in Cerrig.

One day, when both of us were at home, the fire brigade sped past the house and swung into the Maes Aled estate, and Susan remarked half jokingly that perhaps Taid had set his house alight. I went upstairs to have a look, and saw that it was actually Taid's house, and I hurried there at once. The porch and the back kitchen were on fire but fortunately it didn't spread and the firemen soon got it under control. Taid smoked a pipe and he had put it in his coat pocket without checking it properly, and then hung his coat on the back of the chair after he'd been for a walk. The pipe set the coat alight and that's how the fire started!

Taid couldn't really manage on his own. When he lived in Botegir tobacco from his pipe would fall on the floor and he had a habit of throwing spent matches all over the place before they'd been extinguished properly, but that was fine in a kitchen with a slate floor. Maes Aled was different – an old council house with a carpet on the floor that was full of black holes where Taid's tobacco and matches had landed. It was a miracle that he hadn't set the house on fire long before the pipe and coat incident.

Then, one day, he had a stroke. Susan had taken him some food, so she was the first to see him. She immediately called the ambulance and he was taken to St Asaph hospital. He came to but he couldn't speak, and it was obvious to me, and to the hospital staff, that he had lost the will to fight, and that he wouldn't want to live if he was unable to talk. He had enjoyed good health throughout his life. So, having reached the age of 85 years he died, and was buried with Nain in the cemetery in Betws Gwerful Goch. Both of them had been amongst the most important people in my life, two who had been like a mother and father to me.

After Taid's death, the house in Maes Aled was empty, as Haydn had a girlfriend and had moved in with her. So I suggested to Susan who was working in Ruthin by then that we could move from the police station if she so wished. But she didn't want to live in Maes Aled, so we put it on the market and bought Gwynfryn, another house in Cerrig. At the time, many of the council houses were being sold to people from England and elsewhere at inflated prices, but we had the good fortune to buy the house from Glyn Doctor for a fair price when moving from Botegir, and I had no wish to see it being sold to strangers. Haydn agreed, and the house was sold to a local Welshman who was buying for the first time, even though I was offered £3,000 more by an Englishman. So we were able to repay the favour we had received when buying. I may be tight-fisted, but money isn't everything.

During this time, in fact before moving from the police station, the work in the forest was coming to an end, and one day an Englishman who had come to live in Llwyn, Betws Gwerful Goch came by to offer me work. One of my mates, Med Fodwen, already worked for him cleaning water pipes – work that took him far and wide, to Scotland, England and south Wales.

I decided to take the job offered as there was no future for me in the forest. The only drawback was that I had to go where the work was, often far from home. The job was strenuous but interesting, the hours long but the wages good. And it was the kind of work where I could go away on Sunday, work long hours, sometimes all night as well as all day, and come home on a Wednesday night, so it wasn't too bad. The arrangement also suited Med who was a farmer.

The Englishman responsible for the work had invented a very clever machine for cleaning the pipes. It was shaped like a bullet, and we called it the 'Boar'. Our work was to prepare the pipe for the Boar and then replace everything after it had done its job. We cleaned the pipe carrying water from the Alwen all the way to Mold by concentrating on a stretch of two or three miles at a time.

Because the pipe was underground we had to dig to expose it, then isolate a section of it, release the water through the valves from that section creating lagoons in the fields, then make a hole in the pipe to put the Boar inside. Then, we had to control how much water flowed through the pipe in order to drive the Boar forward, moving through the pipe and cleaning it at the same time whilst making a noise like an underground train. We would usually prepare everything during the day and then put the Boar in to clean it overnight, between ten and six, and spend the following day putting everything back in place.

We had to treat the valves and control the pressure with extreme care, because the high pressure of the water made it a highly dangerous job. There were valves all along the pipe, and it was the Water Board's responsibility to ensure that they were opened to let the air out before the pipes were cleaned. It was most important to have the right balance between water pressure and air pressure.

But once, when we were working between Ruthin and Bwlchgwyn, the Water Board failed to ensure that one of the valves above Loggerheads worked properly and things got really messy. The pipe was large, with a diameter of 28 inches, and we put the Boar inside and followed its track above ground. But because the valve hadn't been opened, the air pressure built up inside shattering the pipe and sending tons of water up through the ground, water which then flowed in a torrent down the road. Luckily, there were no cars on the road at the time or they would've been swept away, such was the strength of the water.

It caused £140,000 of damage to the road and the surrounds. We were lucky that it was the Water Board's fault, and they had to pay the bill. But things could have been much worse – there could have been a fatal accident, water pressure and air pressure are very dangerous elements.

It was incredible the amount of dirt we cleared from the pipes, ten tons between Gwernymynydd and Mold, mostly peat as the water came from Lake Alwen. But there was also rust and various other elements. We would take the peat mixed with flouride back to the lakeside, where it was stored for five years, being tested from time to time, prior to being spread on the fields.

I worked for six weeks on a pipe near Pontrhydfendigaid with a lad called Nick Baker, travelling every day, which meant leaving at four in the morning. There was a series of four lakes there, flowing one into the other, and we were cleaning the last three and a half miles between the lowest lake and the new water works. We had to make sure that the pipes to the area's houses and farms were also clear. For that purpose, we would put a two-inch sponge into a one-inch pipe. We also worked locally on the pipe from Arenig to Parc.

We were sent everywhere, wherever there was work to be done, and one time Med and I went to a location near London to clean a pipe that ran underneath the railway line. We travelled there in a lorry, with a tractor and a winch ready for the work. We set off at midnight on Sunday, and Susan was on duty that night. Between Corwen and Llangollen, we saw a police car parked off the road.

'Look', I said. 'Susan's on the lookout for speeding cars. Let's play a fast one on her.' So I started being silly, wobbling from one side of the road to the other, accelerating then slowing down, flashing the lights, bleeping the horn and so on. The car pursued us, blue lights flashing. It overtook us, forcing us to stop.

Then we had a shock, it wasn't Susan in the car but some other policeman that neither of us had seen before! It took quite a lot of persuading before he believed our story. Luckily, he knew Susan and he finally let us go after warning us not to be so bloody stupid the next time.

Having arrived in London, we spent two days preparing the pipe that was to be cleaned overnight. We had to stop every ten minutes when a train came, and we slept for an hour or two at a time in the lorry itself to ensure that no one stole the equipment and the tractor.

On the way home, after travelling through Corwen, we saw a police car by the Goat Hotel in Maerdy. 'Susan,' we said again, and started to tease her once more. Believe it or not, it was the same policeman! Fortunately he saw the funny side of it, and we got away scot-free once again.

I enjoyed my time working on the pipes in places such as Moffat near Newcastle and Denton near Manchester. In Denton, a new pipe was being placed underneath the dual carriageway near a golf course, and it had to be tested to see if it was watertight. The job of welding the pipe was given to a company from France, and the welder was a small Frenchman, no more than five feet tall. He would sit inside the pipe to weld two pieces together. He was the best welder I have ever seen. It was a huge 36-inch pipe and he could weld two sections together without a break, but he refused to weld more than four sections a day because the fumes could endanger his health. I sometimes envied him his job because he received very high wages. He went into the 36-inch pipes and welded them from the inside, and I then followed him on a little trolley like a miner with a lamp on my forehead to clean up after him, and see that everything was right before we closed off the two ends and filled the whole pipe with water to prove it was watertight. And all the time I could hear the roar of the traffic on the road above my head.

But after about three years things suddenly came to an end. Susan was pregnant by then, and I was finding it increasingly difficult to get my wages from the boss. He always had some excuses, and one day, when I went again to ask for my money, he had disappeared – to India apparently, to work with water pipes over there – and he owed me £6,000 which I never saw.

I spent a few months building sheds for Idris Maes Tyddyn, but it wasn't a steady job, and there were no set hours or days. Susan decided that she would return to work after the baby was born if all was well, and so I needed steady, regular work. I went to see Nedw – 'Nedw Fale' (Ned the apples) as he was called, one of the managers at Ifor Williams Trailers, but he had nothing to offer.

However, within a week I received a phone call from Nedw to say he had work for me. So I was employed by Ifor Williams who personally ran the company at that time. He took great interest in his workers and came to me after a week or so to ask how I was getting on. He didn't think I'd last long because I'd been used to working outdoors all my life. But I stuck to it until the accident and it was a pleasure to work for Ifor. He would often tell us that he received more from us than he gave. Then, as he was getting on, his son took over and the company changed after that.

Susan had to go to Glan Clwyd Hospital before our first child was born because she suffered from high blood pressure. Ilan was born on 4 May 1995, and all was well. Susan stayed home for a while, then, when she went back to work, I told her I would give up everything apart from the rugby. Whatever happened I insisted on playing every Saturday afternoon. We hired Beryl Dolhyfryd to look after Ilan, and there was nothing she wouldn't do for him. I would take him to Dolhyfryd by half past seven every morning before going to work and then fetch him home before six in the evening.

It was a pretty tough period for us, and then, after a time, Susan was pregnant again and Teleri was born two years after Ilan on 7 May. Because Susan worked in Bala, we decided to move to the town, if we could find a house that suited us. We needed more space anyway with two children.

Being a policewoman in Bala, Susan was aware of all the comings and goings in the town, and she learnt that Mr and Mrs Roberts, who lived in Tŷ Ni, intended to move to one of the bungalows being built by two local builders, because they found the stairs increasingly difficult. So Susan went to Tom Parry's office and bought Tŷ Ni, and it was a good move because everything became much more convenient for us, although I was sad to leave Cerrig.

iii

Yogi came home on 5 November 2008, and considering what his condition was 18 months ago, no one could ever have imagined that he'd return to Tŷ Ni. When the clouds gathered above our heads on Maes Gwyniad on that fateful Saturday in April 2007, there was no ray of light, no ray of hope. But, miraculously, after everything we had gone through he was home.

I worked like a Trojan to get everything ready for him and, as always with hospitals, it was a last-minute decision to release him. But I was so busy I hardly had time to think what this meant. But when the van appeared at the bottom of the street I could hardly contain myself, I was so excited.

This was what we'd all longed for; this was what we'd prayed for. There had been so many times when it looked as if he'd never be well enough for this, times when it was doubtful if he'd ever live to see this day.

Once he was home the place was like a fairground, and I almost felt as if I was looking on from the outside. Everyone asking how I felt now that Yogi was home, and I wasn't feeling anything at all, just a gaping emptiness inside me.

There was a plausible explanation for this, of course. Some of the hospital staff had travelled with Yogi and the hospital was responsible for him until he crossed the threshold of Tŷ Ni. But once he was home the responsibility rested with the Health Trust. Karen Smith from the High Dependency Unit in Bangor was here, as was Natasha and the carers from Inclusive. Also here were rugby club members, friends and neighbours who had come to welcome him. Everyone was overjoyed to see him.

His homecoming marked the end of a difficult period, but more importantly the beginning of a new and better one hopefully. But I was aware that this period could be even harder to endure. Travelling to Southport as often as I possibly could had been very stressful. The strain of being without Yogi, doing everything on my own, organising the extension and adjustments to the house, all the wrangles with the various Boards to get all that Yogi needed, had taken its toll. But we came through it all thanks to everyone who helped – many have been named in this book and there are many more who have not, but to whom we are forever grateful.

We were now entering a new era, with everyone so glad to have him home, and Yogi of course delighted, but oddly apprehensive at first. It was one thing to long for home from the security of his hospital bed with all the staff and equipment to hand day and night, it was quite a different experience getting used to a new routine with fewer carers and therefore less security, and I know that he felt quite insecure and vulnerable to begin with. After all the excitement, coming home must have been a bit of an anticlimax for him.

Things have changed for me and the children as well, especially with having so many machines in the house and alarm bells ringing day and night whenever there is a crisis. Trying to maintain as normal a family life as possible with carers here 24 hours a day is quite a challenge. But it's worth the struggle to have Yogi home.

He came home in a wheelchair that had to be pushed, but he was more independent when we managed to borrow a better one. One of our first outings was to Tesco's in Ruthin where he careered recklessly round the aisles on the pretext that he was stopping me from buying too much. But I put the brakes on and he couldn't move! A dirty trick I know, but it was the only way to get what we needed. Yogi and speed are a very dangerous combination and I often have to put my foot down. It's amazing how he manages to control the chair with only his chin.

Talking of chairs, so much of his time in hospital seemed to revolve around them, and the many different types he was given. None of them so far have been permanent ones, but hopefully the next one will be.

Over a year ago one of the nurses told him that she'd seen a 4x4 state-of-the-art model advertised by a man from Telford. The saga of who was to pay for it could fill a volume all on its own. To begin with the Health Board said that they would pay and consequently we spent the money we'd earmarked for it on the house. Then they changed their minds in spite of all the letters we and others sent them. Our MP, Elfyn Llwyd, worked hard on our behalf and eventually they decided to pay £10,500, leaving us to find the other £5,500. He'll be like a child with a new toy when it finally arrives.

But the worst problems we've had since Yogi came home is with the agency providing the carers, Inclusive of Chester, who, thank goodness will be finishing at the end of September. Dealing with them has been a nightmare from the beginning, upsetting everyone, especially Yogi. But we're hopeful that things will be much better after September. Yogi has recounted some of the sorry story, so I'll only note what I wrote on the network at the end of June:

> The firm that are looking after Yogi are pulling out before long (GOOD NEWS FOR US!). And we are looking forward to a new beginning. Believe me, things can never be as bad again.
>
> The whole situation since Yogi came home has been totally unacceptable. This firm doesn't seem to appreciate that we are a family and that Yogi and the children deserve respect and stability. I won't go into details; I just want to thank Kate, Mair, Ann and Paula for their dedication and loyalty, hoping they'll be with us for many, many years.

CHAPTER 11

But you are Yogi

i

I WAS A thankless crank when I came home, I know, and I have no excuses for that, but reality was so different to my dreams of home while I was in hospital. All the looking forward, the plans, seeing myself becoming more independent, my family around me and I myself able to go to town once in a while, and taking up the training of the youngsters again in the rugby club.

But it wasn't like that at all. It was difficult to get used to the house because it was so different, it was difficult to get used to the quietness and stillness after the hurly-burly of hospital, and although my family were around me, this could at times be most frustrating. One day Teleri came home from school having injured her leg, and she instinctively expected my usual attention, the attention she needed. She was only eleven and thought the world of her father, her father who in the past could do everything. But I couldn't administer to her needs, I couldn't comfort her, nor cuddle her and give her a kiss as I used to. The children would come in as if nothing had changed and I would become more frustrated every day. Then, after I'd been home for three weeks, Susan returned to work and I was left alone with the carers. I hated to see her go but someone had to fend for us and keep the wolf from the door, and only she could do that.

The main problem was staff shortage, although the company had promised otherwise. The four carers were doing their best and were anxious to do everything properly, and that was putting greater pressure on them. They had no help from the company, not even a list of their duties let alone how to come to terms with being in someone else's house, and they found this difficult at first.

To make things worse I had a bad period with my chest after coming home and that had its effect on the carers and on my own morale. The family had never seen me like this either; they only saw me at my best when they came to visit me in hospital, as I concealed many things from them and rested before they came. But there was no hiding or pretending when I came home and seeing me as I was sometimes scared and disheartened them.

I think that I eventually lost one of my carers because of this – Cheryl or 'Blondie' as I used to call her, the girl from Wrexham, and it was a great loss when she went. She used to work nights and one night my chest was really bad and the ambulance had to be called. Unfortunately the paramedics didn't know what to do. How could they know having never had to cope in an emergency with someone in my condition. Blondie travelled to and from Wrexham on the bus, and wasting an hour and a half night and day was the reason she gave for leaving. But I think seeing me in one of my bad spells frightened her, and I don't blame her for that.

Another one of the six original carers also went fairly soon, one who I think was disappointed with the work, having thought that I would be out every day, going down town or for a stroll, and seeing that I was confined to my home was a disappointment and his work was far from satisfactory.

I had a bad time of it one night and had to be 'bagged', that is air had to be pumped into my lungs with the bag. The carer started doing this and Teleri was sitting on the sofa watching him. He wasn't doing the job properly and Teleri told him so and showed him how to do it. He turned on her and told her to shut up. Then I got mad with him and told him that he wasn't to speak to my daughter like that, especially in her own home. Natasha, the team's manager, was told that his work was unsatisfactory and he had to go.

None of the Inclusive managers came here except for Natasha. She should have been here every day, but she wasn't, and only four carers remained after the other two had gone. It was difficult for them because the company had promised eight carers. Another one who left under a cloud was one of the girls whom I called Jekyll and Hyde, because her work was good but her attitude to her colleagues unfortunate, to say the least. She didn't get on with Natasha either. Two of the carers were on duty on Christmas Day and she was scheduled to come in late and work nights. She rang to say that she wouldn't be coming, and that put extra pressure on the rest of them.

The company then asked another agency, Allied from Colwyn Bay, to provide carers. The problem with them was that they were working in other places as well and there was no knowing how many hours they had been working before they came to me. Two schoolgirls came with the new company, one from Ynys Môn (Anglesey) and the other from Llandygái near Bangor. Laura, the girl from Llandygái stayed until recently, and she was very good.

Christmas came and went. I am not a Christmas person really and it was quite an odd day. Everyone enjoying themselves downstairs apart from me, having fun and playing games whilst I was in my bedroom, going to bed early and watching a John Wayne film. I was pulling everyone's leg accusing them of leaving me alone, but in truth that is what I wanted. I wasn't feeling well, and I know it was unfortunate for Susan because she understood and saw that I was deteriorating rather than getting better. We had agreed to be absolutely open with each other from the beginning, but it is difficult sometimes to say exactly what is on your mind. But I don't think the children guessed anything; they enjoyed themselves.

I got up for Christmas dinner and stayed down for a bit, but I wasn't in a good mood. I was becoming more moody and sad, unable to do anything and not seeing myself getting any better, and the trouble with the carers and the company made things worse.

Natasha promised me new staff after Christmas, and one, Paula from Penrhyndeudraeth, came for an interview. She had previously asked Inclusive for work, but they had done nothing about it. She came in response to an advertisement, although she had never tended to the sick, her work being to help her father in the bake house.

Karen Smith the High Dependency nurse from Bangor and Natasha from Inclusive came to interview her and I was there as well. Since I was well aware of my moods and could offend the carers, I asked her what she would do if I refused to be attended by her, and her answer was: 'If you told me to piss off, I'd piss off'!

Natasha and Karen were absolutely astonished when they heard her answer, but I said that I would be willing to take her on since I needed someone who would give as much as she took, one who was willing to fend for herself knowing that I was a leg puller and often went overboard!

She is still here, as is Kate from Corwen and Mair from Bala. I have a name for each one – Kate is Dyson (Hoover) because she is so good with the suction pump and better than anyone with the blocked pipe. Mair is 'News of the World' because it is from her that I hear all the Bala news, and Paula is Penrhyn Yanker because she tugs so hard at the bedclothes when she makes the bed that the blankets are everywhere.

The three are absolutely marvellous; there are no other words to describe them.

The company contacted Karen Smith in Bangor to say that they wished to opt out of the agreement to provide carers, and she told them to send someone to tell us face to face. But they had to continue for six months, and during that time the contract was advertised and there were five applicants. Then the Health Board decided to run things themselves, and they are in charge since September 2009 although their situation and their name has changed by now.

Soon after the company's announcement, sometime in February, Karen Smith suffered a bad accident near Pentrefoelas when her car was in a head-on collision. She has not been able to work since then.

About the same time Mair suffered a sad bereavement when her husband Ifor died, and naturally I lost her as a carer for a period. I lost the kingpin since she was here from nine to three every day and therefore she was the contact between those who were here in the morning and those who came in the evening. But Mair is Mair and she was back as soon as she could. Then Natasha left the company and there was no replacement, so I had to take over and arrange the rota and sort everything out myself.

Karen's accident and Natasha's resignation were two incidents that left a void in my life and affected me greatly, hardening my attitude. And I found myself asking over and over again why Ifor had to go, was allowed to die, whilst I was still here. Why wasn't I allowed to die instead of suffering like this? I have dark periods like that, thinking that it would be less strain on Susan and the family if I were no longer alive.

But they are also my main reason for living, they and the rest of my family and friends. I don't know what the future holds for me or how much of a future I have, but I am looking forward to getting my new 4x4 chair which is now on its way from Australia. When that arrives, hopefully I can again start training the youngsters and return once again to Maes Gwyniad.

ii

I was 43 in the year 2000, when I moved with the family to Bala, having more or less followed rivers: beginning in Corwen and the river Dee, to Llandyrnog and the Clwyd, Cerrigydrudion and the Alwen, before returning to the Dee more or less at its source in Bala.

Rugby had been an important part of my life long before that of course, at least 15 years before I moved into the town. I didn't realise it at the time, but when I played my first game for Bala, the club had only been in existence for four years. It was formed in 1981 and I joined the club in 1985.

It was therefore a very young club, without any real experience of the game and with no experienced members. The club and we the players learnt as we went along. We trained regularly, yes, but it was fitness training rather than learning the skills of the game. Learning through experience was the only way for me anyway, because I didn't even understand the rules of the game. Some of the other players remember me turning up to play in nylon football shorts which made me stand out from the rest, exactly as happened in Ysgol Brynhyfryd when I wore the Ysgol y Berwyn uniform all those years ago.

My natural instinct on the rugby field was to go for the man every time; and this continued even after I had been taught that the only time to do that was when he had the ball! Indeed I was even guilty more than once of tackling players on my own side. I didn't realise either that the two centres should always position themselves so that one was slightly behind the other. But, despite all these failings, I received an award at the end of the season, the members of the squad having voted me the most promising player.

This was Dilwyn Morgan's opinion of me as a player:

> It was difficult to get it into his head that he was only supposed to be tackling the guy with the ball, and after persuading him of that, he insisted on tackling players from his own side as well. Anyone who happened to be between him and the ball got swept aside quite unceremoniously!

I would often play football for Cerrig in the morning and rugby for Bala in the afternoon, and I was naturally drawn to both. The football crowd tried to persuade me to concentrate on playing for Cerrig, whilst the rugby squad were adamant that I should stick to rugby. I think what tipped the scales for me in favour of rugby was that a number of lads from Cerrig started playing for the club – 'Defaity' and Lynch, Huw Dylan and Ian Cefnbrith, to name a few. That, and also as I have mentioned before, the camaraderie that existed in the rugby club. Whilst playing football I had spent a lot of time by the sea in places like Llandudno and Rhyl and in the Conwy Valley, but the rugby took me to very different places. Another important factor was that Welsh was the language spoken in the rugby club, and my English wasn't all that good then.

There was no second team in Bala when I joined the club; it was formed later and I only ever played for the first team. In those early days we would get thrashed by teams like Blaenau and Bethesda, and we weren't even good enough for teams like Pwllheli and Bangor to consider playing us! We were at the same level as clubs like Dolgellau and Harlech.

I didn't know it at the time, but I had more than one relative in the club. One of them was Hefin Roberts whose father was Taid's brother. He was employed by the Water Board and sadly died when he was just over fifty. He was responsible for the second team when it was formed, getting the lads together and training them. Brian Lloyd Llanfor was another one; both our grandfathers were brothers.

I played in the centre alongside Brian for three or four seasons before moving, as I mentioned earlier, to the pack. I wasn't the fastest centre on the pitch, but as a forward I was fast as they tend to be much slower generally, and speed in the pack is a big advantage. We had a good bunch of forwards when I joined, although I say it myself: Arfon Dalgetty was the hooker; I was loose-head prop and How Rhys Bryn Gwyn the tight-head; Porcyn and Arwel Gwern Biseg in the second row; Bryn Defaity and Euros Puw the two flankers and Emyr Gwern Biseg at number eight.

Slowly but surely the team improved and, at long last, we managed to beat Blaenau. Sometimes we travelled down the A470 to play against teams in south Wales. These trips brought us closer together as a team, but we had this notion that every team in the south was a good one, and it took us a while to realise that, being in the south or not, they were there to be beaten. We played Glyn Coch, a team from the Pontypridd area, twice in one year and beat them both times. They were a very dirty team and Glyn Coch was a very rough area then, and their pitch was in the middle of a housing estate high up on the mountain. The women members of the club raised merry hell after each encounter and their children threw rocks at the bus. They weren't very good losers apparently!

When we went down south, the weekend would often begin on Saturday morning and end on Sunday night. Then, in August, there were the seven-a-side competitions and I would drink many pints before those matches. My drink before the club matches was a pint of Guinness and one whisky, and many of the others had their usual routines as well – Huw Bryngwyn, the scrum-half, for example, drank a tot of rum and water.

Members of the first team kept together wherever we went, staying loyal and supporting each other, and when Gar Lloyd got injured I agreed to replace him as prop. That is when I moved from the centre. The advantage in being a prop was that I could wander anywhere I wanted to on the pitch and follow the ball. I stayed on as prop for some years before making the crucial move to hooker.

Whichever club we visited, the ritual before leaving was the same: we would form a line, go down on our knees and sing 'Hi ho, hi ho, it's off to work we go', the dwarfs' song – only there were 15 of us instead of seven, and not one of us were dwarfs! This never happened when we played at home, we were much more respectable then! I think it was Rhys Jones – Rhys Llandrillo – who started the custom after he'd been playing for Llandudno when he was a teacher in the town. Yes, we were grown men having fun and acting like children.

Bala Rugby Club did not become a full member of the Union for many years, being only an affiliated club. Then, in the mid 1990s, we were assessed by the Union when officials from Cardiff came to visit us to decide if we were ready for senior status. We were far from ready, if only for the fact that we all wore different coloured socks, not to mention the rest of our kit! A rule was passed that everyone was to buy special kit so that we would all be the same, and that we would all pay £2 each for every game we played in order to set up a fund for future use. We changed for matches at Ysgol y Berwyn in those days, and then Euros Puw and 'Gwern Biseg' would take us to Maes Gwyniad – Gwern Biseg in his Land Rover which stank of dog mess!

Small wonder that we remained junior affiliated for some

time until we were eventually accepted and gradually improved as a club, so much so that before the end of the decade we went for two whole seasons without losing a single league match and we won the Gwynedd league four times. We reached the semi-final of the Brewers' Cup once, and were within one match of playing at the Arms Park, but we lost to a team from Llandovery, Cambrian Welfare – a team formed especially to play in the Cup, a team which included some professional players. The Brewers' Cup was played under SWALEC and we had to be assessed before being a part of the competition.

The social aspect of the club was very important and we would arrange various events almost every month. Some members quit when they married, others, like myself and Dilwyn, got married and then carried on. I was 28 when I joined the club and married at 32, much older than most. When 'Defaity' got married, many of the other members who married about the same time left the club.

When I was working away from home on the water pipes, I would travel back from places as far as Newcastle and even London in order to play midweek matches. I only went overseas with the club on one occasion and that was a trip to Ireland with 50 others, enough to form an extra team if needed. The club had been to Amsterdam in 1982, but unfortunately it was before I joined – that would have been an experience! I remember that we arrived at the hotel in Ireland about half past two in the morning, and Dei Peters ran in shouting that the cast of *Coronation Street* was outside as he had seen cars with Granada written on their sides. Some rushed out to see, only to find that they were police cars, with Garda not Granada written on them!

Indeed socialising was very, very important back then, and so was meeting girls. At the hotel in Ireland in 1990 I became friendly with a girl who was a waitress and a cleaner there. I'd been in the bar all night and she came in early to prepare for breakfast, so at the end of her shift I accompanied her back to her quarters, wholly ignorant of the fact that there were eyes watching me leave later that morning. This is how Dilwyn Morgan described the occasion:

> Some of us had gone out early to play pitch and putt on the little course by the hotel. We saw the back door of the building which accommodated the staff being cautiously opened and Yogi coming out with a girl in the doorway waving to him! It was like a scene from a film. He was unaware that we had seen him.

Well, I wasn't married or even in a relationship at the time, so I was a free agent, and I don't think I spent a single night of that trip in my own bed!

During the trip I got into trouble at a hotel in Wicklow when I pulled a flagpole free of its anchor on the lawn and carried it down the path towards the car park, where I almost struck some of the cars because it was much heavier than I had imagined and was difficult to control. I failed to put it back in its place and had to wake Brian Lloyd and Robin Penlan to help me.

Many supporters would follow the team everywhere and for some socialising was more important than seeing the team win. For me, however, winning was everything, winning at all costs. Losing, or even drawing a match after playing well, was no good. But we all made new friends, almost without realising it. I've been amazed at the number of people who have come to talk to me since the accident; people I didn't remember, friends going back 20 years or more.

Every seat in the bus taking us to matches would be taken, especially on trips to the south, but our coaches – Robin Penlan, Bob Tomos and Rhys Jones – decided what we should eat, and while the supporters enjoyed a full cooked breakfast in the hotel, we had to make do with healthier food such as muesli! Bob Tomos was the main coach and it was he who laid down the law and, as we were fit and winning, we succeeded in convincing ourselves that the healthy food was making a difference. Eventually, the first team members had a bus to themselves while supporters travelled on another bus.

For a time rugby became my way of life. I gave up the darts

and going round pubs drinking; I lived rugby, and when I got married, the only thing I didn't give up was rugby. Everything else vanished – rugby and family duties took all of my time.

I have gradually realised in recent years that attitudes towards the game have changed; the dedication isn't there as it used to be. During a hard week of twelve hours a day, I would run eight to nine miles to train, I would travel home late on Friday evening or early Saturday morning, and then on to Machynlleth or Pwllheli or Blaenau to play rugby on Saturday before returning on Sunday back to London or Moffat or Newcastle.

I, along with many others, such as Dilwyn, would refuse to go to a wedding if there was a game on the same day – Euros Puw's wedding, for example, although we did stop by on our way home!

The league system has changed things in north Wales, and the quality of rugby has generally deteriorated. The clubs aren't as socially minded as they used to be either, the feeling of a close intimate family is gone, and the social aspect has declined with the rugby. That's how I see it, anyway. The clubhouses in Bethesda, Blaenau and other places would once be full for hours after a game, as would Plas Coch in Bala. But not anymore – the supporters and team members disperse much sooner than they used to.

But, as I look back, it's good to be able to remember the fun we had – and all I can do now is relive the past. And we did have fun! Wherever we went we had a habit of searching for some souvenir or other to take home with us, and I remember stealing the menu board from outside an Italian restaurant where we'd eaten after playing against Llanelli Wanderers, and bringing it back on the bus to Bala. That night, the restaurant must have phoned before we got back to Bala, as waiting for us there was PC Susan Davies, who was my girlfriend if not my wife by then. But she didn't find the sign, and it stood outside Plas Coch for years. In fact, I suspect they might still have it there now, only that it's been painted over. Susan has been none the wiser as to who was responsible for stealing it, but she will be when she reads this!

No, no one would admit to stealing it, or betray anyone else either. We were as close as a family and Rhys Jones, our boss at the time, would often remind us: 'Don't forget the family.'

The 'family' once went to a very strange place in Cardiff. We rarely went together to international matches, but we went once, and stayed at a posh hotel down in the Bay. Another busload arrived at the hotel and we hijacked the bus and asked the driver to take us to somewhere interesting as we were unfamiliar with the city. We organised a generous collection for him for his trouble. He stopped outside a pub and told us it was a good place. 'Have a good time there, boys', he said as he left us, and we entered a pub full of gay men wearing leather, earrings and all kinds of stuff. They were very friendly – slightly too friendly – and we, from Penllyn and Uwchaled, had never seen such a place. We were shocked, and left in a hurry without our usual 'Hi ho', but cursing the driver who'd played such a trick on us – and accepted a generous tip.

Some of us from the Bala club played for Gwynedd in the Districts' Cup, and we won that, too. There were six of us in the team, more than from any other team in Gwynedd, so we brought the Cup back with us to Bala believing that we owned it. But it should have gone to Bangor, where there were some important men in blazers ready to receive it! As many as seven of us from the club played for Gwynedd during those years. Dilwyn once lost his shirt – he was number 4 and I was number 1. A sub came on the pitch to replace him and as the exchanging of shirts was happening at the end of the game, somehow or other, shirt number 4 went missing, and Dilwyn had to make do with number 24, which meant nothing. Dilwyn never lost his temper, but he did so this time, and it was a sight worth seeing!

He and I weren't far from our 40th birthdays when we played for Gwynedd, and we were lucky to have wives who understood our position – if understand they did! I would place all the blame for being away from home on Dilwyn when talking to Susan,

169

and Dilwyn blamed me when talking to Nia. This worked well and we weren't scared of our wives, unlike some of the others in the club!

We never had any trouble between members in the club, the discipline was remarkable and the pecking order developed naturally somehow. If one member was in trouble, we would make sure he got home safely like everyone else, and the top dog, Rhys Jones, made us all toe the line.

Rugby was a way of life, and when I brought the family to Bala, I realised how many advantages there were compared with my time with the Cerrig football team where I was outside the inner circle. Here in Bala I took part in all the arrangements and as I worked in Cynwyd, barely ten miles away, I also had plenty of time on my hands.

I would usually finish work at a quarter past four, and overtime never went beyond six o'clock. Early enough to go down to Maes Gwyniad. And if I arrived home earlier to look after Ilan and Teleri when Susan was working late, I would take them down with me. I went about the place cutting the grass and cleaning the clubhouse while they played on the field.

Eventually, they were both keen to play rugby themselves, so I was roped in to train the juniors and it was a pleasure getting to know the young children and their parents. In fact the training sessions were more like crèches to begin with, as the parents would disappear after bringing their children to the session but, little by little, I managed to draw them in as well – to help with arrangements and to join us when we visited other clubs. This worked fine with children under the age of 13, but the older kids didn't want their parents with them!

Alan, who lived next door, was in charge of youth football training in the town, and I helped him, and he helped me. As the children grew older, more and more teams were formed, until eventually we had five teams, from U-9s to U-16s.

Everything was going well and I was delighted to be able to give the new generation some of the advantages that I didn't have when I was their age. And then, on a sunny spring day in

April 2007, came the fateful scrum, and within the space of ten seconds or less, it all came to an end for me, and my life, and the life of my family changed completely.

iii

Christmas was the first major event after Yogi's homecoming and back in 2008 I'd promised him a day to remember when he came home. This would be our perfect opportunity to celebrate the fact that he was well enough to take his place as head of the family again.

But having read Yogi's version of how he felt you'll know that this wasn't how it was at all. The root cause of the problem was his condition. He wasn't in the best of spirits and he had a rotten Christmas Eve. I knew he was struggling and making the effort to appear cheerful for the children's sakes and mine. I also think he felt a bit low watching me preparing everything such as wrapping the children's presents, one of the things he used to do before his accident. Knowing that he would never do these things again was heartbreaking for him.

He didn't feel well on Christmas Day and it was a tremendous effort for him to come down to lunch, but that's Yogi all over, he didn't want to disappoint the children. The effort tired him out and he went to bed early.

But, to strike a more positive note, one of the amazing successes of the last two years is the fund that the rugby club started, a fund that is nearing the quarter of a million mark, the fund that is absolutely essential to our lives.

You must forgive me, I've mentioned the fund several times already, but its success has made such an impact on us and being able to have Yogi home is so dependent on it. The amount raised reflects the unbelievable goodwill towards him from all directions and it instigated over the two years so many different events and activities: three parachute jumps, many marathon races and sponsored cycle races, concerts and auctions, games of all sorts and sponsored walks, all this as well as large and small donations from individuals. Schools and chapels, pubs, clubs and societies from all over Wales and beyond contributed, and as a family we can never acknowledge enough the amazing kindness extended to us.

I've mentioned before that Yogi's care and treatment is financed by the Health Authority and the Welsh Health Commission, but the structure in Wales has changed recently, and several Trusts have been set up, including the Betsi Cadwaladr Trust which is responsible for this area.

But the fund paid for all the building work on the house, including the lift, and that alone cost £200,000. But the costs would have been much higher were it not for all the volunteers who put in so much unpaid labour. Glyn Lloyd from Cerrig, Gwyn Roberts, Rhosygwaliau and Llion, Lôn Llanuwchllyn did all the roofing so that only the slates had to be paid for. We were responsible for the electrical work but the firm of contractors, Faulkner, didn't charge us for labour. Cwmni'r Gro Sarnau supplied us with loads and loads of cement, Travis Perkins reduced their price to us and there were many other generous contributions to the work.

And thankfully the efforts to raise money are still going on; the money is still coming in as are the bills. It costs £600 annually to insure the van, £450 to service it, £50 to insure his present wheelchair and it will be in the hundreds when he gets the new one, and having to maintain his temperature at 37 degrees means that the heating bills have more than trebled.

Following a feature in the *Daily Post* and an interview I had with 'Jonsi' on his Radio Cymru programme, more money came in to boost the fund and I must mention two donations. A 95-year-old gentleman from Denbigh, Emrys Evans sent £200 and the same amount came from a lady in Bangor.

Years ago when I was 14, I went to Germany with a group from Coleg y Bala. Our leader was Dafydd Owen, no longer with us unfortunately, and one of the boys in the group, one I remember well, was Dafydd Arthur Jones from Bangor. Several years ago a young man died while walking near Trefriw in the Conwy Valley, his picture was in the paper and I recognised him. It was Dafydd Arthur and it was his mother who had sent the £200. Rather than writing to thank her I phoned and we chatted for three quarters of an hour. She said she no longer sent Christmas cards but sent a donation to charity and she wanted the money to go to Yogi's fund this particular year. She'd suffered a terrible loss, the loss of an only child, and talking to her was quite an emotional experience for me, maybe because I'd known Dafydd Arthur when I was young. As Yogi always says, what goes around comes around.

Chapter 12

Seeing through the clouds

EVERYONE HAS HIS say in our house, so it's only right that it happens in this book as well. So here's a chance for everyone, and I'll have the last word!

Teleri

The first time I saw Dad in the hospital I ran out screaming because I was so shocked and frightened to see him as he was, but that was only the first time. After that, I looked forward to seeing him every Saturday, and sometimes on Sunday too. It was often difficult to fit everything in, because I had a lot of homework and a lot of harp and piano practising to do. But it was much easier during the holidays.

I became friendly with many of the staff members in Southport, and we would all have fun with them and some of the other patients too, and I'm still in touch with some of them online. I also used to look forward to Dad's jokes – he always had something funny to say.

One difficult aspect after he came home, especially at the beginning, was people asking me all the time how Dad was, as if he had been ill and was going to recover. But he isn't ill, he had a terrible accident and he isn't going to get any better, this is how he will be for the rest of his life. But fewer and fewer people ask the question now, having come to terms with the reality of the situation.

When he came home it was difficult to get used to the carers being present all the time, though they had their own room. They were in the house 24 hours a day, and I had to struggle to be myself. Some of them got under my skin and wouldn't let me be alone with Dad, not realising that Ilan and I knew what to do and how to treat him when necessary. I had to tell one or two of them that I wanted time alone with Dad and that I was responsible enough. We know each other better by now and the best carers are the ones still with us: Mair, Kate, Ann and Paula. But there are also new carers coming in now with the new company, and it will take time for us to get used to them, and them to us.

It was also difficult to get used to all the machines that are here, especially when they made a noise if something went wrong. I am a light sleeper and wake up every time one of them bleeps during the night. If it goes on for a long time I know that Dad's in pain and I have to go to him.

It's great to have him home, and not having to go to Southport all the time, but better still having him to comfort us when we need comforting, and to help Ilan and me with our homework. He cheers us up, reminds us of things we need to do, and gives us tips. He reminds me to practice the harp, piano, sax and guitar. Usually, we both see him between quarter to and quarter past eight every morning, before we're off to school, and it's easier now that the new company has started to manage things.

In the evening, we're allowed to come and go as we like, and we usually eat supper together in the bedroom at about seven as he goes to bed early. Sometimes he stays in bed in the morning and then goes to bed later than usual in the evening. When that happens, he comes downstairs and we have our supper there. But wherever we eat it's a time for us to be together as a family, to share experiences and news, who we met and what happened during the day. And although Dad has been in his room all day whilst the rest of us have been out, it is he that does most of the talking!

I realise that I've had to grow up quicker than others of my age, because I've had to take more responsibility. Most of what Ilan and I do for him goes some way to pay back for all he did for us. He used to run for us, now we run for him. And I have to do myself the things he did for us, like running a bath, sorting dinner money, go shopping in town, the everyday chores that have to be done.

I have a passion for rugby, it's my main interest, and I've got that from Dad. The accident hasn't changed my attitude towards the game at all, and I want to find a team I can play for. I train regularly and Mam just tells me to be careful. I have other interests as well, but it's mainly rugby.

Bala is a close community and we're very lucky to live here. But sometimes people get under my skin when they complain about small things, such as feeling a little stiff or something. At those times I want to tell them that Dad doesn't complain, even though he has every right to, and that they should try to imagine how it feels not to be able to move at all. Sometimes I do say something and regret it later, but sometimes I bite my tongue.

I'm lucky to have good friends who are close and have been with me through everything, such as Elin Hedd, my best friend. I can tell them how I feel and they are ready to listen and give me their support.

Ilan

I didn't run out when I saw Dad for the first time in the hospital, although it was a shock to see him with the tubes all around him, especially the one in his mouth. He was in Wrexham then.

I enjoyed going to Southport and made friends with the staff. I once went swimming with one of the nurses' children, and Teleri would have come too if she hadn't shut the car door on her finger. And it was she who did that, as I often remind her, she can't blame anyone else. I enjoyed going for meals to the Richmond, a hotel near the hospital. The food was nice there and we didn't have to pay; Mam paid – with Dad's card!

I used to get fed up with people asking how Dad was as if he were ill. But I know what they were trying to ask, just that their words didn't come out right. The ones that have been coming to see Dad know exactly what the situation is, and they never ask if he's better.

One thing that made me a little bit jealous to begin with was seeing other children's fathers able to take them to the rugby, while there was no-one with me. Dad always used to take me.

When he came home it was difficult to begin with, especially with the carers everywhere. But most difficult of all was having to accept that he was home but unable to play football and wrestle with me. What he used to be able to do he can now only say. He says and I do.

My opinion of him has changed. Before the accident I thought at times that he was completely stupid, but I know now that he's not. He knows a great deal, there's a lot in his head and he's a huge help to Teleri and me with our school work. I study Technology at school and neither I nor Mam knew what things like dove tail joints were, but Dad knew and could explain them to me.

I'm used to the carers by now. There are two of them here all the time, and at night one is asleep and the other awake. It can be difficult for us as a family as they are here full time, but it's difficult for them too – maybe even more so.

If there is a minor crisis, one carer can solve it, and sometimes Mam helps, but if things are bad the other carer has to be alerted as well. I never hear the noise of the machines bleeping as I'm a deep sleeper. One night there were two ambulances outside during the small hours and someone asked me at school the next day what they were doing there. I had no idea, as I had slept through everything.

When Dad's in pain he acts tough and pretends that things aren't as bad as they really are. I respect that, but worry at the same time.

It's nice not having to go to Southport all the time, but what pleases Dad is that less money is spent on petrol! At the same time, he's worried that the electricity bill is so high and complains about that. But the house must be kept at a constant temperature.

Teleri and I have to fend for ourselves much more than we used to, although Mam does more for us as well. But she's very busy, working full time, keeping house, a governor at school and she sings with the choir. When she has an evening meeting we have to take more responsibility for supper; heating it, peeling potatoes or boiling pasta, things like that. And if Mam's too busy to take me to the rugby ground, I walk, as I always do when I go to the Leisure Centre, which is good for me.

When I was ill in bed, Dad would look after me and do the simple things like opening the window or getting me a drink. I'm able to pay him back now by doing the same things for him.

Dad's interest in rugby is the same as ever. He wants to get back to being a coach and everybody else wants him back too. He took us to Pwllheli recently when we were playing against the youth teams of that area – Pwllheli and Botwnnog.

When Dad was injured, Mam told us both to stop playing rugby. But she was upset, and now she says that it's our choice, and she supports us in every way. I can't help but being interested in rugby – rugby, rugby, rugby is everything: on television, the Bala Rugby Club, the Welsh team. And the greatest thing that could happen to me would be to play for Wales.

Dad has always nurtured a good attitude towards the game in every player he has coached. He would tell us as youths that it didn't matter what the score was, that the important thing was to try our best and that learning to lose was also essential. It's important to lose with dignity and to win without rubbing it in. After each game he would ask 'Have you learnt something'?

Some teams get angry after losing, but Bala don't. The team's attitude has been good, and a lot of that's because of Dad. It's important to be friendly with the other team, and to forget every rivalry on the pitch once the game is over. He always had a very important saying: 'Whatever happens on the pitch stays on the pitch.' Dad has always preached this.

When he came home, I had a negative attitude to everything,

thinking of all the things Dad wouldn't be able to do; that he would be completely different to how he was before the accident. That's true to some degree, but he can do much more than I had imagined, and he's given me a lot of confidence. Before the accident, his main contribution was physical, now it's mental, and he's as precious to us as ever.

I've been very fortunate in my friends as well, they've been behind me a hundred percent, and I'm able to tell them how I feel.

Teleri and I are very lucky to have Mam; without her, what would we do? Other members of family have been supportive as well, especially Nain and Taid Caernarfon – Dick and Morfudd. They've been fantastic, and continue to be. Joyce, Dad's sister, and Dei her husband as well; they've been excellent and still come here regularly. During the last two years Dad has been through hell, but he's fought against all the adverse circumstances, and he's still fighting.

Susan

When Yogi was 50 he received a card from Gwion Lynch containing this *englyn* (a stanza in strict metres):

> A'r haul wedi mynd i rywle – drwy'r haf
> Nid yw'r hwyl fel bydde,
> Ond ti yw Yogi, ynde?
> Mi weli drwy'r cymyle.

(The sun having disappeared somewhere all summer, the mood is not what it was. But you are Yogi, aren't you? and being Yogi, you will see through the clouds.)

I know nothing about the *cynghanedd* (strict metre) of the *englyn*, but to me it's perfect, and describes our situation perfectly. Yes, the sun did disappear from our lives on Maes Gwyniad in April 2007 and there have been more clouds than sunshine since then. But Yogi is a fighter, and even though he's had his low periods, he fights his way through them because that's who he is.

We are settling down to regular family life once more, and I'm now the only bread winner. The children are pupils in Ysgol y Berwyn and are growing up through everything – especially their clothes! As they grow their father and I can depend more and more on their companionship and support, and they have an extremely mature attitude. Yogi is home and is an essential member of the family, and even though he can't do anything physically, his mind is as healthy and sharp as ever. I long sometimes, when things are dark, for him to be able to put his arms around me to comfort me. I miss that more than anything but he is here to discipline, to listen, to suggest, to advise. The fact that he survived such a horrible accident is a miracle. We are still holding on to that miracle.

Myself

On 29 September, two years and a half after the accident, I went down to Maes Gwyniad on training night. There were 14 kids of different ages there with Llinos Gwanas coaching them. I had coached some of these kids myself, so they knew me well. But some of the younger kids were staring at me in wonder, and I asked them what they thought of me in a wheelchair. They didn't say anything, but after about 15 minutes they started to forget themselves and began to talk, asking about the chair and various other things.

I got a lot of pleasure from being there, but my voice was weak, so I'll have to learn to shout again or get a megaphone or something. It'll be easier when I have the new chair, the 4x4.

By now there are at least seven people coaching: Dr John and Huw Dylan from Llangwm, Alan from next door, Bethan and Martin from Frongoch, Gethin Caerau and Llinos Gwanas, and Tony himself of course. He's still there and as keen as ever. I may have mentioned Tony by more than one name – well, he's called Tony Parry as the chairman of the club, Tony if he's done something wrong, and TP when he needs to put his hand in his pocket at the bar! He's been one of my most loyal friends.

Six months after the accident, I received a letter from

Brendan McNutt who had been head of Bryn Melyn, Llandderfel, an organization for children with attitude problems as a consequence of maltreatment, many of them having offended. He played for Bala's first team when he was in the area. This is an extract from his letter:

> ...Of course you had a strong, fit and able body, but so did all the other players. What set you apart was your attitude; the strength, not only of your muscles, but of your character, your unstoppable spirit. That spirit has always been inside you and it will always be there... it is who you really are.

The spirit is low at times, yes, especially when there's trouble with my neck, but he's probably telling the truth as I was accepted to Southport on the condition that I had in me the will to fight to get better, and I've done that throughout the whole time. I've had enough time to think, too, and perhaps Brendan McNutt can express my feelings better than I can:

> One of the toughest things for every man to learn in life is to be compassionate with himself... to forgive himself for sometimes not being his best... Being kind to ourselves is part of being great and is also essential if we are to be kind to the others in our life. Yogi, I have no idea what life is like for you, but I hope that you create a life that you enjoy and that enables you to express yourself without reserve.

The final paragraph of this book is in danger of becoming an acknowledgment address, but I have so many people to be grateful to: Susan and the children more than anyone, they have supported me through thick and thin and are my main reason for continuing to fight; other members of my family who have already been named; the hundreds of friends, acquaintances and benefactors who poured their goodwill and fundraising efforts in my direction; the amazing staff at the hospitals; the carers; and everyone who has supported me and continue to do so.

What does the future hold for me? Who knows, but Brendan McNutt's letter utters the hope that I'm creating for myself a life I can enjoy and through it to express myself. With the help of all around me, I'm trying.

Postscript

IN SEPTEMBER 2009 Betsi Cadwaladr Health Board took over my care package. They promised more trained carers to look after me, but the promise was never kept. The High Dependency nurse failed to turn up to do the training half the time. My health started to deteriorate throughout the month of October, and because of their concern, my carers at the time rang the Health Board to inform them, but no-one took any notice. I asked for physiotherapy but they told me that I had to have an infection or pneumonia before they could provide it. By the beginning of November I was feeling quite rough. Oh, I thought, another cold on the way.

November 20th, 2009 saw the launching of the original Welsh version of this book at the Plas Coch Hotel in Bala, and an excellent evening it was. Following the launch I was confined to my bed for six weeks and in January 2010 my ventilators and humidifier didn't operate properly. The constant converting of water into steam in order to lubricate my throat was essential, but when things went wrong the pipes had to be cleaned and drained every half hour because the equipment was gradually drowning me.

The High Dependency Unit at Bangor was contacted but they refused to send anyone out to investigate, so we got in touch with the hospital at Southport and arranged a short visit there. That was January 2010 and I came home again in January 2012, the short visit having lasted two years and two days, longer even than my previous stay there!

After an investigation it was found that I had a collapsed lung, a fact which the Health Board should have discovered and I was told at the hospital that I wouldn't have survived for longer than another fortnight. It was a lucky chance that the humidifier failed and that I went to Southport. For two to three months they tried reflating my lung, but failed, and it was finally decided that I would have to survive on one. All the equipment was readjusted accordingly.

This period affected me mentally. We'd had a lot of trouble with the Health Board after it took over care responsibility from the private company, and as I was back in hospital the board sacked the carers.

Towards the end of 2010 I asked if I could have the collapsed lung removed, and a specialist from Liverpool came to assess the situation. Deliberations continued for three months before it was decided that the operation would be too risky, although I was willing to take the chance. So by March 2011 there wasn't much more that could be done, I was in a stable condition and ready to return home. But I had no carers and the Health Board was not interested in seeing me home. It was costing them £1,100 to keep me in hospital; much less than the cost of supporting me at home. So, it was in their interest that I stayed in Southport.

But I was a problem, because I was bed blocking, and there were urgent cases needing attention. What the hospital did was to raise the weekly fee to £4,400 and, as a result, the Health Board was immediately interested in getting me home.

Luckily for me, Southport eventually found a private company, Spirit Care, willing to take the responsibility and it has proved to be an excellent choice. Finally a package was agreed with them, and Tess Cunningham and Sheila Bowden came to see me on behalf of the company. Tess is in charge of running the house and because she and the company listened to what I wanted, it has been easier for me to be home because I have everything done my way.

This time all my carers are local, however I have difficulty in remembering their names so I have given them all 'nicknames', and here goes. I'll start with the noisiest, Rambo (because she throws me all over the bed), and Dobbie (because she wouldn't listen to the master, like Harry Potter), Posh Spice (because she has a double-barrelled surname). The other three left under a cloud and I still don't know what I did to upset the married couple, 'the Hammers' who left.

So now I have three new carers, suitably nicknamed Leaky (because she punctured the plastic bag that carries water to the dehumidifier), Boo Boo (because she thinks she's Yogi's best friend), but it hasn't worked out that way because I only have associates! The next one is Half Pint (because she is so short she could walk under an ironing board without bending). Then there is Diveboard (because she slipped on some water and landed on top of me on the bed, and I have a very broad smile). Last but not least is Whiplash (and I'll leave that to your imagination – car). I now need to complete my team of ten.

Getting back to the serious stuff, now I have two weekly physio sessions that help keep my right lung clear, and the staff also give me physio on my chest twice a day, and this makes a big difference to my breathing.

Finally my wheelchair arrived after two years of waiting, partly paid for by the Welsh Rugby Charitable Trust and partly by private donations. I am now mobile and can be seen around town and down on Maes Gwyniad. I am involved there with the building of an extension to the clubhouse and a restaurant where the children and all those who train can relax after training, it's a restaurant without alcohol.

I have spoken to hundreds of people since I returned home but oddly enough, no one has ever asked me what I miss most following my accident. The answer is sex! Susan has read the 'Shades of Grey' books and says that they don't get close to what our sex life was like before the accident. Ha Ha!

The children are growing and developing in leaps and bounds. Ilan was greatly honoured when he was selected to carry the Olympic Torch on one stage of its journey around Wales, and Teleri was chosen as one of a dozen or so out of hundreds of applicants to go to Malawi for a fortnight to do charity work. They were accompanied by the S4C film unit and the result was a series of programmes illustrating the youngsters' involvement with the people of Malawi. She is becoming an independent person with great interests in raising money for various charities, including doing a bungee jump and also a parachute jump on a cold wet day, jumping from ten thousand feet in aid of Air Ambulance Wales. I have seen the video and watching it made me scared stiff.

Susan has had a hard time in the last two and a half years. Not only is she still a police officer, she has carried the family on her own for the last six years, and during that time she has been told three times at least that I was going to die, and the burden of doctors telling her one thing and me bouncing back like a rubber ball has finally caught up with her. At the moment she is off work with stress and depression, which is not surprising after everything she has been through. It takes time to get over that sort of illness but I think she can see a light at the end of the tunnel.

*

On Friday, 30 August, 2013, Bryan Davies passed away at his home in Bala. His funeral was held at Maes Gwyniad, Bala.

Susan

I have no intention of having the last word in this book because Bry (as I always addressed him) wanted to have the last word.

My husband, my best friend, my soul mate quietly passed away at home in the company of myself, Ilan and Teleri on the evening of Friday, 30 August this year (2013). Bry had not been well for some months but continued to live life to the full until the very end. Despite his pain and suffering (which he faced on a daily basis), he never complained and was always thinking of others. There will always be a huge void in our lives without this remarkable man at our side, to advise us and to guide us though life. What I do know is that he will live in our hearts for ever and I am sure as time goes by, the pain we feel because of our loss will ease and the memories will give us comfort.

One of the last things Bry made me do before his death was to post the final transcript of this book. I am so glad he managed to see it through as in years to come the next generation of our family can read about the life of this remarkable man that we were privileged to have known. I hope this book will also be of comfort to others that are facing life with severe physical disabilities.

Bry left a letter on his laptop detailing his funeral wishes. I therefore give him the last word by sharing with you the letter he left us. This follows a tribute by Teleri to her father.

Hero

It's still in my mind as if it happened yesterday. My father away from home. There are many reasons why a child's father would be away from home. Mother and father separated? No, not my parents. Their love is as strong as ever. A father fighting for his country in a foreign land like Afghanistan? No, not my father, even though he is away fighting his own battle.

My father's biggest love is rugby (except for my mother should I say?); he breathed and lived for rugby.

April 21, 2007, was the day that changed our lives. My father, my mother, my brother and me.

My father walked through the front door, his smile as wide as ever, his muscular body could be seen through his shirt and his walk as energetic as ever. It didn't cross my mind that it would be the last time I would see my father walking and moving his arms; the last time I would have his strong arms wrapped tightly around my small body. Worst of all that he wouldn't be returning home for a year and a half.

My father and I are like best friends. We stick together through thick and thin. We laugh together and cry together. He is my hero for many reasons.

I have many memories with my father. The time we spent together playing outside, our family holidays and, of course, the time we spent together on the rugby field cutting the grass.

I never thought one day my perfect life would change. It was a Saturday morning. My father had a rugby match as he had every Saturday. Before the match my father announced that he was retiring from the game and that today would be his last game. He was given the important role of captain. He marched the team onto the field, their heads held high. Five minutes into the game my father was left seriously injured. He had broken his neck.

The first time I visited my father in hospital I ran out hysterically, my mind in absolute turmoil, the uncomfortable-looking collar around his neck, the never-ending pipes. His eyes shut, no communication, no answer, he was induced in deep sleep… in a coma. His body was as still as Bala Lake on an icy day. I never thought that I would see my father in such agony. My inside was like unsettled jelly as a cold breeze ran down my spine and a cold sweat ran down my forehead. I could feel my eyes filling up with water.

I was only nine years old when my father had his accident. A young girl with high expectations. I didn't realise that it would be a process of maturing years for my brother and I. We didn't realise it would be life-changing experience for the whole family. I remember the words of the medical consultant: "He is lucky to be alive. It will be a life changing. He hasn't only lost the use of his legs but also his arms. We think that he won't be able to move his head, talk or eat again…" his soft voice faded away. We didn't know what to say. Was this possible?

Luckily, as time passed by slowly, my father proved the medical consultant wrong. He was able to move his head, to talk and eat. The future didn't look as dark after all.

Sometimes I lie in my bed trying to imagine how my father feels. Free mind trapped in a body that you don't have control over. Life can be cruel sometimes.

My father was in local hospitals for the first few weeks until he got moved to a hospital that specialised in back injuries in Southport. We visited him regularly, the two-hour journey seemed like it was getting longer and longer.

What about the future? We take one day at a time. You never know what's around the corner. We will always fight our own war as a family, but we will always have each other.

Wherever my father is, however my father is, he will always be my father. My hero.

Teleri Davies

My Funeral

I would like someone to read this letter out.

I would like Porcyn and Huw Dylan to organise a small service at the rugby ground.

I would like Huw Dylan to read the Welsh version because his Welsh is better than mine!

I would like Porcyn to read the English version so that I can have one last laugh at his expense.

I would like Arfon Dalgetty and Hyw Rhys to carry the front of my coffin from the car to the field so that the best front row that ever played for Bala can be together for one last time.

I would like Ilan Wyn and Al Prys to carry the back so I can feel as though I am standing for one last time.

I would like, if possible, for the old Rhys Jones Choir to sing a couple of songs. The people I remember include Huw Bryngwyn and his brother Hyw, Euros and Iolo Pugh, Dalgetty, Alwyn Ambiwlans, Porcyn, Huw Dylan, Gwion Lynch, Dewi Disgarth, Daf Tŷ Cap, Gwyndaf Hughes, Brian Lloyd, Robin Penlan, Eryl Vaughan and Bryn Defeity. I know there were many more, so I hope they'll all join in.

The songs I want them to sing are 'The Yogi Bear Song' and 'Calon Lân'. The last song is the Welsh Anthem 'Hen Wlad Fy Nhadau'.

I would like Ilan Tŷ Newydd and Llŷr Aeddren to start the singing because they were the ones who made the biggest fuss when they found out I was going out with Susan.

I need to thank so many people.

I would like to thank the people of Penllyn for making me and my wife and kids so welcome when we first moved to Bala. I made many new friends and I still have many good old friends after all this time.

Everybody knows that rugby brought me to Bala… and the person you have to blame for this is Robin Penlan. Like Susan

189

used to say "Saturdays are for grown men wanting to be children for a couple of hours."

I won't start naming people I need to thank for fear of offending... but I do need to mention all the rugby clubs, all the social clubs, schools and individuals that have raised money or donated in anyway that enabled me to come home.

I need to thank the three hospitals that brought me back from the dead, especially the nurses within the special care units. There are nurses that I have to name from Southport: Alison King, aka Smiler! She saved my life three times. Helen Kremar who allowed me into her family and carried all the pies into the ward! Elaine Fairlamb, for all the great arguments we had. The ginger bombshell called Kellie, who gave me a few kicks up the backside but has a heart of gold.

I need to thank all at Spirit Care for looking after me since coming home. Thank you Tess for allowing me to have my own way – ALWAYS! To Aaron for allowing me to take control of the rota; you have to admit that I was better than you at understanding the rolling rota! To ALL that gave me the best care possible at home – past and present staff: Mair, Kate, Anne (Half a Scouser) to name a few of my past... and to the end, Ange (Rambo), Morwenna (Dobbie), Rhian Eds (Whip-lash), Mel (Dive Bomber), Pauline, Chris, Lisa and David. You all stuck with me through thick and thin – the good and not so good days. I will be forever grateful to you all.

Thank you also to Siôn and staff at the chemist – my medication list was longer than most shopping lists! Also to Dr Robin for his mutual respect and to all his staff. To Joy for her weekly Thursday visits, the natter and not forgetting the physio bit!

I would like to thank all the children I have met over the years. It's been a joy to see them develop within the game and in life, in general, and to see them mature into young gentlemen... and ladies, of course!!

One person I need to thank is Tony Parry for all the running around he has done over the past six years. The one time I will never forget was the time I turned up for his 50th birthday party. I have never seen him speechless before!

Last but not least I need to thank Teleri, Ilan and Susan. Except for them I would never have survived the last six years. They went to hell and back for me. It has been harder for them than for me.

I am glad that I have had the time to see them grow up into really good and intelligent young adults. All I hope is that they do what they want to do in life and to live life for themselves.

And last… there are no words to explain what Susan has done for me over the 23 years we have been together. She has carried the family from the day we got married to today. So now it's time for her to enjoy life without me hanging around her neck and depending on her so much in the last six years. I only ever told her that I loved her three times in the past 23 years we have been together… like I used to say "If I didn't love you I wouldn't have stayed."

I WANT TO THANK YOU ALL FOR COMING TODAY and if I have missed anyone out… it was not my intention to offend.

My cremation will be strictly private… as I don't trust Tony Parry anywhere near fire after his unfortunate accident at the rugby field last year!

It is my wish for all donations to go towards building a canteen for the younger members of the rugby club.

The Scrum that Changed my Life is just one of
a whole range of publications from Y Lolfa.
For a full list of books currently in print, send
now for your free copy of our new full-colour
catalogue. Or simply surf into our website

www.ylolfa.com

for secure on-line ordering.

TALYBONT CEREDIGION CYMRU SY24 5HE
e-mail ylolfa@ylolfa.com
website www.ylolfa.com
phone (01970) 832 304
fax 832 782